AF791589

Hollington on Shareholders' Rights

HOLLINGTON ON SHAREHOLDERS' RIGHTS

First Supplement to the Ninth Edition

Up to date to 4 November 2022

ROBIN HOLLINGTON KC, MA (Oxon), LLM (Penn.)
Bencher of Lincoln's Inn

SWEET & MAXWELL

THOMSON REUTERS

Published in 2022 by Thomson Reuters, trading as Sweet & Maxwell.
Thomson Reuters is registered in England & Wales, Company No.1679046.
Registered Office and address for service: 5 Canada Square, Canary Wharf, London, E14 5AQ.

For further information on our products and services, visit
http://www.sweetandmaxwell.co.uk

Computerset by Sweet & Maxwell.
Printed and bound by CPI Group (UK) Ltd, Croydon, CR0 4YY.
A CIP catalogue record for this book is available from the British Library.
For orders and enquiries, go to:
http://www.tr.com/uki-legal-contact; Tel: 0345 600 9355.

ISBN (print): 978-0-414-11093-9

ISBN (e-book): 978-0-414-11097-7

ISBN (print and e-book): 978-0-414-11095-3

Crown copyright material is reproduced with the permission of the Controller of HMSO and the Queen's Printer for Scotland.
Precedent material in this publication may be used as a guide for the drafting of legal documents specifically for particular clients, though no liability is accepted by the publishers or authors in relation to their use. Such documents may be provided to clients for their own use. Precedents may not otherwise be distributed to third parties.

All rights reserved. No part of this publication may be reproduced, or transmitted in any form, or by any means, or stored in any retrieval system of any nature, without prior written permission, except for permitted fair dealing under the Copyright, Designs and Patents Act 1988, or in accordance with the terms of a licence issued by the Copyright Licensing Agency in respect of photocopying and/or reprographic reproduction. Application for permission for other use of copyright material, including permission to reproduce extracts in other published works, should be made to the publishers. Full acknowledgement of the author, publisher and source must be given.

Thomson Reuters, the Thomson Reuters logo and Sweet & Maxwell® are registered trademarks of Thomson Reuters.

FSC
www.fsc.org
MIX
Paper | Supporting responsible forestry
FSC® C013604

© 2022 Robin Hollington

Previous Editions

First Edition	1990
Second Edition	1994
Third Edition	1999
Fourth Edition	2004
Fifth Edition	2007
Sixth Edition	2010
Seventh Edition	2013
Eighth Edition	2017
Ninth Edition	2020

Preface to the First Supplement to the Ninth Edition

The 9th edition attempted to state the law as at July 2020. The intervening period has been marked by the disruptions and lock-downs occasioned by the Covid-19 epidemic. But the civil legal system, in contrast to its criminal counterpart, was one of the few activities that was able to continue to function reasonably well. Court filings took place online. Remote conferencing facilities came into their own, with meetings and court hearings taking advantage of the modern technology that was available. Lawyers would sit at home, dressed in business or court dress from the waist up, and pyjamas and slippers below! Now that things have returned to something resembling normality, there is a lingering wistful nostalgia for the convenience of remote conferencing facilities.

There have been few judgments of major significance, and no changes in the relevant statutory framework, since the publication of the 9th edition. This Supplement nevertheless summarises the many judgments which have appeared during this period in this field. A brief summary is set out on the back cover of this Supplement.

Apart from my quasi-miraculous transformation from a QC to a KC upon the death of Her Late Majesty the Queen this year, I would highlight the following developments of major significance:

- In July this year the new *Business and Property Courts of England & Wales Chancery Guide 2022* came into force. It states:

  > "*1.14* This is the first new edition of the *Chancery Guide* (the '*Guide*') since February 2016. Much has changed since that time and the *Guide* has been wholly re-written to take account of changes in the way that the Chancery Division courts operate, technological changes, and new practices that have evolved, particularly during the Covid-19 pandemic.
  >
  > *1.15* Work has been carried out to seek to align the content of this *Guide*, the *Commercial Court Guide* and the *Technology and Construction Court Guide* where practices in the Chancery Division and in those courts should be substantially the same, though there are many areas of practice that are different and where different guidance is appropriate. ..."

- Very recently the Court of Appeal handed down its judgment allowing the appeal in *Re Compound Photonics Group Ltd* [2022] EWCA Civ 1371, reversing [2021] EWHC 787 (Ch) (Adam Johnson J). This is an important decision upon the issue of duties of good faith owed between shareholders and is discussed in para.4-39 and elsewhere in this Supplement. I must disclose my interest in that case, appearing as I did for the petitioners who lost the appeal.

I announced my retirement at the end of 2020 at the end of the trial in *Re Compound Photonics Group Ltd*, but the appeal in that case has kept me in practice. I am glad, however, to have found in the meantime Mr. Adrian Pay, a colleague of mine in chambers throughout our respective careers, to take over the editing of this work. He has done all the hard work in preparing the contents of this Supplement, although, as authors say, I take ultimate responsibility for it, and all the opinions, and, more importantly errors, are mine. Adrian has been my overworked junior in many major shareholder disputes over more years than I care to remember, and I know he is a safe pair of hands.

I would also like to express my thanks to the editorial staff at Sweet & Maxwell, and particularly Callie Leamy, for their expert and friendly assistance in the production of this Supplement.

I have tried to state the law, in England at least, as at 4 November 2022.

Robin Hollington KC
Lincoln's Inn
2 November 2022

How to use this supplement

This is the first supplement to the ninth edition of *Hollington on Shareholders' Rights*, and has been compiled according to the structure of the main work.

At the beginning of each chapter of this supplement, a mini table of contents of the sections in the main volume has been included. Where a heading in this table of contents has been marked with a square pointer ■, this indicates that there is relevant information that is new to the Supplement to which the reader should refer.

Within each chapter, updating information is referenced to the relevant paragraph in the main volume.

TABLE OF CONTENTS

TABLE OF CASES

TABLE OF STATUTES

TABLE OF STATUTORY INSTRUMENTS

CHAPTER 2

Broad Principles

TABLE OF CONTENTS

THE RULE IN FOSS V HARBOTTLE—THE DERIVATIVE CLAIM AND CONSTRAINTS IN EQUITY

Principle 12—"Fraud on the minority" exception to Principle 10: The derivative claim

The statutory code

Replace list item "(4)" with:

(4) The procedure for the bringing of a statutory derivative claim is now governed by CPR rr.19.9–19.9F and Practice Direction 19C—Derivative Claims. **2-20**

CHAPTER 3

Majority Rule

TABLE OF CONTENTS

DIVISION OF ROLES BETWEEN BOARD OF DIRECTORS AND SHAREHOLDERS

Principle 7—Shareholders' control

Replace the second paragraph with:

The shareholders are the owners of the company and therefore in ultimate control since they appoint and remove directors. The directors will act in breach of their duty to exercise their powers for proper purposes if they fail to observe "the constitutional distinction between the respective domains of the board and the shareholders": per Lord Sumption in *Eclairs Group Ltd v JKX Oil & Gas Plc* [2015] UKSC 71; [2016] B.C.C. 79 at [16], [37]; see *Re Baker & Metson Ltd* [2022] EWHC 1988 (Ch) at [204]–[212], [271]; and *Barrowfen Properties Ltd v Patel* [2021] EWHC 2055 (Ch) at [268]–[272], [292]; see also paras 5-31–5-32. **3-03**

After the second paragraph, add a new paragraph:

However, the articles of association and any supplemental shareholders' agreement will invariably provide for a division of roles by entrusting management powers to the board, and, apart from those regulating the appointment and retirement of directors, the provisions of the company's constitution may on their true construction protect directors from interference by the shareholders in the execution of the management functions entrusted to them. But it is clear that the shareholders have certain residual powers flowing from their ultimate control over the affairs of the company, such as the power to ratify and waive breaches of fiduciary duty by the directors, and the power to act where the directors are unable or even unwilling to do so.

Right to inspect the company's books and records

To the end of the second paragraph, after "[2017] B.C.C. 387", add:

3-05 ; *Houldsworth Village Management Co Ltd v Barton* [2020] EWCA Civ 980; [2020] B.C.C. 953, CA

Replace the paragraph with:

3-07 In contrast, a director does have a common law right to inspect all the company's books and records: they need this right in order to carry out their duties as a director properly[3]: *Conway v Petronius Clothing Co Ltd* [1978] 1 W.L.R. 72 Ch D; *Dilato Holdings Pty Ltd v Learning Possibilities Ltd* [2015] 2 B.C.L.C. 199; *Re Premiere Care Holdings Ltd* [2021] EWHC 1595 (Ch); *Chu Chung Ming v Lam Wai Dan* [2014] HKEC 2132; *Hammond v Quayeyeware Pty Ltd* [2021] FCA 293; s.388(1) of the 2006 Act. In general, it makes no difference that the director is also a shareholder: indeed, the very reason for a shareholder having representation at board level is to confer such a right of inspection. A director's common law right to inspect the books and records of the company is, however, qualified by the restriction that the right must be exercised for the purpose of carrying out his duties as a director: *Oxford Legal Group Ltd v Sibbasbridge Services Plc* [2008] Bus. L.R. 1244.[4] In that case a petitioner claiming relief on the unfair prejudice ground, which had a nominee on the board, sought to obtain wider disclosure of documents than was available in the petition proceedings by procuring its nominee director to commence separate proceedings. The crucial factor militating against the grant of interim relief to the claimant was the fact that the petitioner had agreed to sell its shares and the only remaining issue in the petition was that of valuation.

[3] Compare a director's right to information with a partner's right to information: *Inversiones Frieira SL v Colyzeo Investors II LP* [2012] Bus. L.R. 1136 at [26]–[28].

[4] The judgments in *Berlei Hestia (NZ) Ltd v Fernyhough* [1980] 2 N.Z.L.R. 150 also repay detailed consideration. See *Tsai Shao-Chung v Asia Television Ld* CACV 185/2011; [2012] 4 HKLRD 52, for the court's reluctance to impose conditions upon the exercise by a director of his right to inspect company's records. See also *Dilato Holdings v Learning Possibilities* [2015] 2 B.C.L.C. 199; *Chu Chung Ming v Lam Wai Dan* [2014] HKEC 2132; *Yung Siu Wa v Raffles Family Office Ltd* [2018] 5 HKLRD 816 (inspection refused where director intending to bring unfair prejudice proceedings).

CHAPTER 4

The Bargain between Shareholders

TABLE OF CONTENTS

PRINCIPLE 16—GOOD FAITH IN LAW AND EQUITY

Replace list item "(1)(c)(ii)" with:

(1) (c) (ii) a contractual duty of "good faith", whether express or implied, means that, whilst the obligor cannot act having regard *solely* to his personal interests, he need only have due regard to the interests of his obligee; and **4-04**

ORDINARY RULES OF CONTRACT

The process—express and implied terms

Replace paragraph with:

As held by the Supreme Court in *Marks & Spencer Plc v BNP Paribas Securities Services Trust Co (Jersey) Ltd* [2016] A.C. 742, the interpretation of a contract is a different process from the implication of a term in it: the two are different processes governed by different rules; it is only after the process of interpretation of the words of the agreement has been completed that one turns the issue of implication: per Lord Kitchin in *Wells v Devani* [2019] UKSC 4 at [28]. The significance of this is that Lord Hoffmann had stated that the issue of whether to imply a term into a contract was "one of construction of the agreement as a whole in its commercial setting": cited in the passage below from the speech of Lord Neuberger in the *Marks & Spencer* case. For the extra-judicial debate between Justices of the Supreme Court, see lecture of Lord Sumption, "A Question of Taste: The Supreme Court and the Interpretation of Contracts", The Supreme Court, May **4-10**

8, 2017; and an article by Lord Hoffmann in (2018) L.Q.R. 553. In the *Marks & Spencer* case, Lord Neuberger, with the intention not so much of refuting that statement as a general proposition but to stop it from undermining the limited nature of the court's power to imply terms, observed:

"25. The second point to be made about what was said in *Belize Telecom* concerns the suggestion that the process of implying a term is part of the exercise of interpretation. Although some support may arguably be found for such a view in *Trollope & Colls Ltd v North West Metropolitan Regional Hospital Board* [1973] 2 All ER 260 at 268, [1973] 1 WLR 601 at 609, the first clear expression of that view to which we were referred was in *South Australia Asset Management Corp v York Montague Ltd* [1996] 3 All ER 365 at 371, sub nom *Banque Bruxelles Lambert SA v Eagle Star Insurance Co Ltd* [1997] AC 191 at 212, where Lord Hoffmann suggested that the issue of whether to imply a term into a contract was 'one of construction of the agreement as a whole in its commercial setting'. Lord Steyn quoted this passage with approval in *Equitable Life* [2000] 3 All ER 961 at 970 , [2002] 1 AC 408 at 459, and, as just mentioned, Lord Hoffmann took this proposition further in *Belize Telecom* at paras [17]–[27]. Thus, at para [18], he said that 'the implication of the term is not an addition to the instrument. It only spells out what the instrument means'; and at para [23], he referred to: 'The danger ... in detaching the phrase "necessary to give business efficacy" from the basic process of construction.' Whether or not one agrees with that approach as a matter of principle must depend on what precisely one understands by the word 'construction'.

26. I accept that both (i) construing the words which the parties have used in their contract and (ii) implying terms into the contract, involve determining the scope and meaning of the contract. However, Lord Hoffmann's analysis in *Belize Telecom* could obscure the fact that construing the words used and implying additional words are different processes governed by different rules.

27. Of course, it is fair to say that the factors to be taken into account on an issue of construction, namely the words used in the contract, the surrounding circumstances known to both parties at the time of the contract, commercial common sense, and the reasonable reader or reasonable parties, are also taken into account on an issue of implication. However, that does not mean that the exercise of implication should be properly classified as part of the exercise of interpretation, let alone that it should be carried out at the same time as interpretation. When one is implying a term or a phrase, one is not construing words, as the words to be implied are ex hypothesi not there to be construed; and to speak of construing the contract as a whole, including the implied terms, is not helpful, not least because it begs the question as to what construction actually means in this context.

28. In most, possibly all, disputes about whether a term should be implied into a contract, it is only after the process of construing the express words is complete that the issue of an implied term falls to be considered. Until one has decided what the parties have expressly agreed, it is difficult to see how one can set about deciding whether a term should be implied and if so what term. This appeal is just such a case. Further, given that it is a cardinal rule that no term can be implied into a contract if it contradicts an express term, it would seem logically to follow that, until the express terms of a contract have been construed, it is, at least normally, not sensibly possible to decide whether a further term should be implied. Having said that, I accept Lord Carnwath's point in para [71] to the extent that in some cases it could conceivably be appropriate to reconsider the interpretation of the express terms of a contract once one has decided whether to imply a term, but, even if that is right, it does not alter the fact that the express terms of a contract must be interpreted before one can consider any question of implication.

29. In any event, the process of implication involves a rather different exercise from that of construction. As Sir Thomas Bingham trenchantly explained in *Philips* [1995] EMLR 472 at 481:

'The courts' usual role in contractual interpretation is, by resolving ambiguities or reconciling apparent inconsistencies, to attribute the true meaning to the language in which the parties themselves have expressed their contract. The implication of contract terms involves a different and altogether more ambitious undertaking: the interpolation of terms to deal with matters for which, ex hypothesi, the parties themselves have made no provision. It is because the implication of terms is so potentially intrusive that the law imposes strict constraints on the exercise of this extraordinary power.'

30. It is of some interest to see how implication was dealt with in the recent case in this court of *Aberdeen City Council v Stewart Milne Group Ltd* [2011] UKSC 56, 2012 SLT 205, 2012 SCLR 114. At para [20], Lord Hope described the implication of a term into the contract in that case as 'the product of the way I would interpret this contract'. And at para [33], Lord Clarke said that the point at issue should be resolved 'by holding that such a term should be implied rather than by a process of interpretation'. He added that '[t]he result is of course the same'.

31. It is true that *Belize Telecom* was a unanimous decision of the Judicial Committee of the Privy Council and that the judgment was given by Lord Hoffmann, whose contributions in so many areas of law have been outstanding. However, it is apparent that Lord Hoffmann's observations in *Belize Telecom* at paras [17]–[27] are open to more than one interpretation on the two points identified in paras [23]–[24] and [25]–[30] above, and that some of those interpretations are wrong in law. In those circumstances, the right course for us to take is to say that those observations should henceforth be treated as a characteristically inspired discussion rather than authoritative guidance on the law of implied terms."

Interpretation of the words of the agreement

Textualism v contextualism—ambiguity and business common sense

Replace the second paragraph with:

In *PM Law Ltd v Motorplus Ltd* [2018] EWCA Civ 1730 at [12], Asplin LJ gave this summary: **4-12**

> "It is common ground that the court's task when construing clause 1 of the 2007 Agreement is to ascertain the objective meaning of the words used by the parties in the context of the 2007 Agreement as a whole, taking into account the relevant factual background which would have been available to the parties, but excluding subjective evidence of the parties' intentions. The court must focus on the meaning of the relevant words in their documentary, factual and commercial context. If there is an ambiguity, or in other words, there are rival meanings, the court can give weight to the implications of the rival constructions by reaching a view as to which is more consistent with business common sense: *Arnold v Britton & Ors* [2015] AC 1619 per Lord Neuberger PSC at [14]–[23] and *Wood v Capita Insurance Services Limited* [2017] AC 1173: [2017] UKSC 24 per Lord Hodge JSC at [8]–[15]."

After the second paragraph, add new paragraphs:

In *Arch Insurance (UK) Ltd v Financial Conduct Authority* [2021] UKSC; 1 [2021] A.C. 649, in summarising the principles of contractual interpretation as discussed in *Wood v Capita Insurance Services Ltd* [2017] UKSC 24; [2017] A.C. 1, it was held at [47]:

> "The core principle is that an insurance policy, like any other contract, must be interpreted objectively by asking what a reasonable person, with all the background knowledge which would reasonably have been available to the parties when they entered into the contract, would have understood the language of the contract to mean."

Cf. *EMFC Loan Syndications LLP v The Resort Group Plc* [2021] EWCA Civ 844; [2022] 1 W.L.R. 717 at [56]–[58], per Asplin LJ, as a summary of the principles to be derived from *Rainy Sky SA v Kookmin Bank* [2011] UKSC 50; [2011] 1 W.L.R. 2900; *Arnold v Britton* [2015] UKSC 36; [2015] A.C. 1619 and *Wood v Capita Insurance Services Ltd* [2017] UKSC 24; [2017] A.C. 1173.

In *Glenn v Watson* [2018] EWHC 2016 (Ch) at [183], Nugee J drew attention to the emphasis placed by Lord Hodge in his above statements of principle on the relevance of the quality of drafting in question:

> "These include his statement that textualism (a close examination of the relevant language in the contract) and contextualism (the factual background known to the parties, and the implications of rival constructions) are not conflicting paradigms but tools which can be used to ascertain the objective meaning of a contract; and his repeated statement that the quality of the drafting can affect the readiness of the Court to have regard to the wider context: see at [10] *('the court must … depending on the nature, formality and quality of drafting of the contract, give more or less weight to elements of the wider context')*, [11] *('in striking a balance between the indications given by the language and the implications of the competing constructions the court must consider the quality of drafting of the clause')* and [13] (*'The correct interpretation of other contracts may be achieved by a greater emphasis on the factual matrix, for example because of their informality, brevity or the absence of skilled professional assistance'*)." (Emphasis in original.)

In a nutshell, the better the drafting, the more emphasis will be given to textualism over contextualism in the interpretation of the contract. Yet where there has obviously been a mistake in the drafting, the court must be satisfied as to the nature of the necessary correction before it is able to ignore an express term of the contract: see *Parker v Roberts* [2019] EWCA Civ 121. Where it was argued that an event had subsequently occurred which was not contemplated in the language used in the contract, the court was not entitled to disregard the language unless it was clear not only that the event was not contemplated but also what the parties would have intended in that eventuality: see *Astor Management AG (formerly MRI Holdings AG) v Atalaya Mining Plc (formerly Emed Mining Public Ltd)* [2018] EWCA Civ 2407.

ARTICLES OF ASSOCIATION

Pre-emption provisions

To the end of the third paragraph, add:

4-22 But see *Re Euro Accessories Ltd* [2021] EWHC 47 (Ch) (a right of compulsory expropriation in the articles at "fair value" construed as connoting a discount for a minority shareholding); and similarly *Agbaje v The Robert Frew Medical Co Ltd* [2022] EWHC 1373 (Ch) (a deemed transfer notice pursuant to a shareholders' agreement at "fair market value" construed as connoting a discount for a minority shareholding).

A COLLATERAL SHAREHOLDERS' AGREEMENT

After the first paragraph, add a new paragraph:

4-33 In *NDK Ltd v HUO Holding Ltd* [2022] EWHC 1682 (Comm) it was held at [48]–[53] that articles of association and a shareholders' agreement should be construed together, with the one being part of the admissible background to the other. In that case a dispute resting on the articles (no jurisdiction clause, governed by Cypriot law as place of incorporation) was subject to the exclusive jurisdiction agreement in the shareholders' agreement (English law, LCIA Arbitration). Contrast, the decision of the Singapore High Court in *BTY v BUA* [2018] SGHC 213.

DUTY OF GOOD FAITH IN CONTRACT

Implied term

After the first paragraph, add new paragraph:

Cf. *Pakistan International Airline Corp v Times Travel (UK) Ltd* [2021] UKSC 40; [2021] 3 W.L.R. 727 at [27] per Lord Hodge "... in contrast to many civil law jurisdictions and some common law jurisdictions, English law has never recognised a general principle of good faith in contracting." **4-37**

Content and breach of duty of good faith

After the first paragraph, add a new paragraph:

See also *Astor Management AG v Atalaya Mining Plc* [2017] EWHC 425 (Comm); [2017] Bus L.R. 1634; *Bates v Post Office Ltd* [2019] EWHC 606 (QB); *New Balance Athletics Inc v Liverpool FC* [2019] EWHC 2837 (Comm); *Soteria Insurance Ltd v IBM United Kingdom Ltd* [2022] EWCA Civ 440. **4-39**

After the last paragraph, add a new paragraph:

The meaning and content of an express contractual duty of care has been reviewed in the important recent judgment of the Court of Appeal in *Re Compound Photonics Group Ltd* [2022] EWCA Civ 1371, reversing [2021] EWHC 787 (Ch) (Adam Johnson J). Upon the occasion of the substantial equity investment made by the investment vehicles of Russian oligarchs, rendering the current shareholders a minority, professionally drafted new articles of association and a shareholders' agreement were put in place, which included an express duty of good faith in the latter. There were other provisions which required the two named continuing directors, one of whom had founded the business and the other of whom had introduced much of the old equity capital, to be part of the majority of any decision of the board and therefore in effect appeared to give them a veto over board decisions. The trial judge interpreted the good faith clause in the context of the articles of association and shareholders' agreement as imposing three duties upon the majority shareholders: a duty of fidelity to the bargain which prevented the majority from removing the two named directors; a duty of fair and open dealing; and a duty to take into account the interests of the minorities. He went on to hold that the majority shareholders had ridden roughshod over these duties in a number of respects. The Court of Appeal, reversing the trial judge, and distinguishing and disapproving a variety of dicta in first instance and Australian cases, held that the duty of good faith in a shareholders' agreement such as this entailed no more than a duty owed by the majority shareholders of honesty and to refrain from sharp practice. The Court referred to the decisions of Leggatt J (as he then was) in *Yam Seng Pte Ltd v International Trade Corp Ltd* [2013] EWHC 111 (QB); [2013] 1 All E.R. (Comm) 1321 and of Leggatt LJ (as he had become, but still sitting in the High Court) in *Al Nehayan v Kent* [2018] EWHC 333 (Comm); [2018] 1 C.L.C. 216, in effect finding that the express duty of good faith in the case before it meant the same as the implied duty of good faith in the latter case. There was no impediment to the right of the majority to remove the two named directors—had any such impediment been intended by the parties, it would have been expressly provided for and it would have been enforceable by injunction. The Court of Appeal emphasised the special nature of the relationship between shareholders in a company governed by the Companies

Act 2006 as one where it was axiomatic that no duties of good faith were owed. Commenting on the concept of "fidelity to the bargain" to be found in many of the authorities including the previous decision of the Court of Appeal in *Re Coroin Ltd* [2013] EWCA Civ 781; [2014] B.C.C. 14, Snowden LJ held:

> "[212] ... [E]ven where thought to be inherent in an obligation of good faith, the concept of fidelity to the bargain or adherence to the spirit of the agreement could only operate to support the common purpose and aims of the parties as objectively ascertained from the express or implied terms of the contract. Depending on context, the essence of the concept might be captured by Barrett J's reference in *Overlook* to the prohibition of 'cynical resort to the black letter' or by Allsop P's reference in *Macquarie* to the prohibition of conduct that 'undermines the bargain entered or the substance of the contractual benefit bargained for'. On any footing, however, the shared aims of the parties must be identified by interpretation of the other terms of the agreement, or by implication of terms according to the usual test outlined in *Marks & Spencer plc v BNP Paribas Securities* [2016] AC 742.
>
> [243] ... [A]part from the 'core' duty of honesty and (depending on the context) a duty not to engage in conduct that could be characterised as bad faith, any further requirements of an express duty of good faith must be capable of being derived as a matter of interpretation or implication from the other terms of the contract in issue in the particular case."

CHAPTER 5

Directors' Duties

TABLE OF CONTENTS

THE NEW STATUTORY CODE FOR DIRECTORS' DUTIES AND ITS RELATIONSHIP WITH EXISTING LAW

Duties owed to creditors

In the second sentence of the second paragraph, after "in a number of cases, most recently", replace "BTI 2014 LLC v Sequana SA [2019] B.C.C. 631." with:

5-10 *BTI 2014 LLC v Sequana SA* [2019] EWCA Civ 112; [2019] B.C.C. 631 (appeal to Supreme Court pending).

After the quote in the second paragraph, add a new paragraph:

In *Barrowfen Properties Ltd v Patel* [2021] EWHC 2055 (Ch) at [281]–[283], it was held that the duty to consider the interests of creditors entailed considering the interests of creditors as a whole, as well as potentially the interests of particular creditors where relevant. Further, the duty to consider the interests of creditors entailed only that the director in question honestly believed that his act or omission was in the interests of creditors.

RELEVANCE OF BREACH OF DIRECTORS' DUTIES TO THE STATUTORY OPPRESSION REMEDIES

In the first paragraph, after "but see also Ch.10, paras 10-14–10-15 below.", add:

5-11 (The passage above was accepted as a "succinct and accurate summary of the law" in *Re Gallium Funds Solutions Group Ltd* [2021] EWHC 765 (Ch) at [58]).

RATIFICATION OF DIRECTORS' BREACHES BY THE MEMBERS

The "Duomatic" principle—unanimous consent of all shareholders

After the first paragraph, add new paragraphs:

5-13 The "*Duomatic*" principle was considered by the Privy Council in *Ciban Management Corp v Citco (BVI) Ltd* [2020] UKPC 21; [2021] A.C. 122 at [31]–[47]. There, a BVI company with bearer shares had been acquired for the purpose of concealing assets—certain parcels of land—of a businessman, B. The company had a corporate agent and corporate director, which were accustomed to act on the instructions of an associate, C, of B who had been assisting B in the concealment of the assets. C procured the company, through its corporate agent and director, to issue a power of attorney to him so as to sell the land and C used the proceeds of sale to pay debts which he alleged to be owed by the company to him. B had given actual authority to C to instruct the director to issue earlier powers of attorney, such that those became acts of the company through the *Duomatic* principle. It was held that, as respects the power of attorney in question, C's ostensible authority, in that B had set up a mode of operation whereby the agent and director were expected to take C's instructions as having been provided with B's authority, was sufficient for the purposes of the *Duomatic* principle. Further, although it was a requirement of the *Duomatic* principle that there was no relevant dishonesty, that requirement was not engaged: the granting of the power of attorney did not involve dishonesty by either B or the director (notwithstanding that the purpose of the corporate structure was to conceal assets) and even if C had acted dishonestly that was the very risk which the structure which B had set up entailed, such that B could not complain of it as against the director, which he expected to act in accordance with C's instructions.

See further *Satyam Enterprises v Burton* [2021] EWCA Civ 287; [2021] B.C.C. 640 at [40]–[60] and *Byers v Chen* [2021] UKPC 4; [2021] B.C.C. 462 at [62]–[72].

To the end of the last paragraph, add:

Cf. *Ciban Management Corp v Citco (BVI) Ltd* [2020] UKPC 21; [2021] A.C. 122, similarly, as respects ostensible authority, as discussed above

After the last paragraph, add a new paragraph:

Cf. *Satyam Enterprises v Burton* [2021] EWCA Civ 287; [2021] B.C.C. 640 at **5-14** [46]–[55] (a transaction at an undervalue to a sole shareholder could amount to an unlawful return of capital so as to prevent the operation of the *Duomatic* principle).

Replace the paragraph with:

In general, the relevant knowledge and consent for this purpose is that of the **5-15** registered shareholder, regardless of any persons beneficially interested in the shares, on the principle that the company cannot look behind the register or inquire as to the trusts affecting shares: *Inland Revenue Commissioners v Bibby* [1945] 1 All E.R. 667 at 671.[20] Where, however, the beneficial owners of shares have the requisite knowledge and give the requisite approval, they cannot subsequently rely upon the ignorance of the legal owner: *Deakin v Faulding* (2001) 98(35) L.S.G. 32 Ch D per Hart J. See now *Ciban Management Corp v Citco (BVI) Ltd* [2020] UKPC 21; [2021] A.C.122 at [47]:

> "… in some cases doubts have been expressed as to whether the principle applies where it is the beneficial owners, rather than the registered shareholders who consent ... But the correct view is that, at least as here where the ultimate beneficial owner, and not the registered shareholder is taking all the decisions in the relevant transactions, the *Duomatic* principle applies as regards the consent of (and authority given by) the ultimate beneficial owner."

[20] See also *Domoney v Godinho* [2004] 2 B.C.L.C. 15, *Re Kilnoore Ltd (In Liquidation)* [2006] Ch. 489 and *Dickinson v NAL Realisations (Staffs.) Ltd* [2019] EWCA Civ 2146. For a discussion of this issue, see Peter Watts, "Informal Unanimous Assent of Beneficial Shareholders" (2006) 122 L.Q.R. 15.

THE DUTY OF GOOD FAITH

General principles

After the first paragraph, add new paragraphs:

In *Ma Wai Fong v Kie Yik* [2022] UKPC 14; [2022] B.C.C. 953, it was held that **5-26** where there has been a failure by a director to consider the separate interests of the company (there, in contra-distinction to the interests of a wider group of family companies), the test is whether the director could, in the whole of the existing circumstances, have reasonably believed that the transaction was for the benefit of the company (thus, absence of separate consideration does not, of itself, mean that there was a breach of duty).

In *Barrowfen Properties Ltd v Patel* [2021] EWHC 2055 (Ch) at [276], it was observed that it is no answer to a claim for breach of s.172 that the director believed himself to be acting in the commercial interests of the company if he knew or believed that he was not acting fairly between the members.

Replace footnote 34 with:

5-27 [34] *Fairford Water Ski Club Ltd v Cohoon* [2020] EWHC 290 (Comm) at [51] (not affected on this point by *Fairford Water Ski Club Ltd v Cohoon* [2021] EWCA Civ 143; [2021] B.C.C. 498); *Lehtimaki v Cooper* [2020] UKSC 33; [2022] A.C. 155 at [232].

THE DUTY TO EXERCISE POWERS FOR A PROPER PURPOSE

General principles

Replace footnote 36 with:

5-31 [36] See *Re Last Lion Holdings Ltd* [2018] EWHC 2347 (Ch); *Stobart Group Ltd v Tinkler* [2019] EWHC 258 (Comm) at [426]–[452]; *Fairford Water Ski v Cohoon* [2020] EWHC 290 (Comm) at [51]. Cf. *Financial Technology Ventures II (Q) LP v ETFS Capital Ltd* [2021] JCA 176 at [48]–[49].

From the end of the second paragraph, delete "In Eclairs Group Ltd v JKX Oil & Gas Plc [2016] B.C.C. 79, Lord Sumption (with whom Lord Hodge agreed) held that the court had to focus on any improper purpose that the board had in exercising the power and ask whether the decision would have been made if the board had not been moved by that improper purpose: see at [21]."

After the penultimate paragraph, add a new paragraph:

5-32 In *Re Derbyshire Aggregates Ltd* [2021] EWHC 2455 (Ch), the court was satisfied that a director/shareholder ensured that the company did not pay a sizeable dividend in order to apply pressure on his fellow shareholders in negotiations for the sale of his shares, breaching his duty to act in good faith and for proper purposes, and thus unfairly prejudicing them pursuant to s.994 of the Companies Act 2006.

Replace the last paragraph with:

In *Eclairs Group Ltd v JKX Oil & Gas Plc* [2016] B.C.C. 79, the Supreme Court held that a power under the articles to impose restriction notices on shareholders who did not comply with a disclosure notice under s.793 of the 2006 Act had to be exercised for a proper purpose—the fact that the addressee of the notice had only himself to blame for his default was immaterial. Lord Sumption, with whom the rest of the Court agreed on this point, offered the following important guidance at [37] as to the mischief at which "the proper purpose rule" (as he described it at [15]–[31] was aimed:

> "The rule that the fiduciary powers of directors may be exercised only for the purposes for which they were conferred is one of the main means by which equity enforces the proper conduct of directors. It is also fundamental to the constitutional distinction between the respective domains of the board and the shareholders. These considerations are particularly important when the company is in play between competing groups seeking to control or influence its affairs ... But there is nothing particularly special in this context about a decision to issue a restriction notice under a provision such as art.42. The directors' task is no more difficult than it was in the many cases like *Howard Smith Ltd v Ampol Petroleum Ltd* [1974] AC 821 in which other fiduciary powers, such as the power to issue shares, have been held improperly exercised because in the face of pressures arising from a battle for control the directors succumbed to the temptation to use their powers to favour their allies. I would agree with the majority of the Court of Appeal that in that situation the board would naturally wish to have the predators disenfranchised. That is precisely why it is important to confine them to the more limited purpose for which their powers exist. Of all the situations in which directors may be called upon to exercise fiduci-

ary powers with incidental implications for the balance of forces among shareholders, a battle for control of the company is probably the one in which the proper purpose rule has the most valuable part to play."

After the last paragraph, add new paragraphs:

So, it is a breach of the proper purposes duty for directors to use their powers to control or influence the outcome of a general meeting: *Re Baker & Metson Ltd* [2022] EWHC 1988 (Ch) at [204]–[212] and [271]—*sed quaere* whether this is too broadly expressed, e.g. since directors also have a duty to keep shareholders properly informed (as to which see Principle 6(14) and para.5-76). See *Barrowfen Properties Ltd v Patel* [2021] EWHC 2055 (Ch) at [268]–[272] and [292] for discussion of the proper purpose rule, concluding that a director could not properly exercise his powers to prevent shareholders from appointing other directors or to prevent those directors from exercising their powers, even if the director considered that to do so was in the best interests of the company.

Two linked issues have continued to be controversial since the decision of the Supreme Court in *Eclairs Group*:

(a) Does the "substantial purpose" test import a "but for" causation, i.e. there will be a breach of the duty if but for the improper purpose the power would not have been exercised? See *Re Baker & Metson Ltd* [2022] EWHC 1988 (Ch) at [212].
(b) What if the directors have mixed or multiple purposes?

In *Re Cardiff City Football Club (Holdings) Ltd* [2022] EWHC 2023 (Ch), it was held that one director had mixed purposes when authorising a new allotment of shares, one of which was legitimate—viz. to improve the company's financial position—but the other of which was improper—viz. an expectation that the offer of shares would benefit the majority shareholder and dilute specifically the shareholding of a particular minority shareholder, an aim which the majority shareholder wished to achieve. The judge followed the analysis of Lord Sumption in *Eclairs Group Ltd v JKX Oil & Gas Plc* [2015] UKSC 71; [2016] B.C.C. 79, making a distinction between the lawfulness of the decision and its consequences, holding that the director acted in breach of duty but the decision of the board would have been the same had the director in question not been affected by the improper purpose and thus the decision could not be said to have been unfairly prejudicial to the petitioner.

In the British Virgin Islands, the 'substantial or dominant purpose test' has been followed: *Antow Holdings Ltd v Best Nation Investments Ltd* [2018] ECSCJ No.253 (September 21, 2018); *Nam Tai Property Inc v IsZo Capital LP* [2021] ECSCJ No.714 (October 4, 2021). In *Amstel Investment Holdings Ltd v AMS Holdings Ltd* BCIHVMAP2021/0016 (November 8, 2021), it was held that the fact that a decision of the directors may have, or had, as one of its effects the benefitting of one group of shareholders over another does not mean, without more, that it was made for an improper purpose and thus invalid. It is a question of fact as to whether the decision was made for an improper purpose, in the sense that such effect was the substantial or dominant effect.

THE DUTY TO EXERCISE INDEPENDENT JUDGMENT

General principles

In the third paragraph, after the first sentence, ending "at [62]–[68], [147]–[149].", add:

5-41 Cf. *Re Cintep Development Ltd* [2020] EWHC 3210 (Ch) at [306]–[308].

To the end of the penultimate paragraph, after "the company's accounts", add:
and *Byers v Chen* [2021] UKPC 4; [2021] B.C.C. 462 at [91]–[94]

After the penultimate paragraph, add a new paragraph:

In *Re Cardiff City Football Club (Holdings) Ltd* [2022] EWHC 2023 (Ch), the Court rejected a claim that directors had not exercised independent judgment. The fact that draft board minutes had been prepared in advance did not give rise to the inference that independent judgment was not exercised at the meeting. Even though one director was found to have reached a decision for partially improper purposes (see para.5-31) so as to breach his s.171 duty, that did not entail a breach of the s.173 duty: see [105] per Adam Johnson J:

> "… It is perfectly possible, it seems to me, for a company director, acting independently, to form the view that the company's best interests are achieved by implementing just the same proposal as is favoured by the company's majority shareholder, who has been responsible for appointing that director. Such a coincidence of interests is not unusual, and the fact that it existed in this case does not, I think, enable me to conclude that Mr Dalman failed to act independently."

THE DUTY TO AVOID CONFLICT OF INTEREST AND DUTY

The statutory code—no conflict

After the last paragraph, add a new paragraph:

5-48 The above observations stand qualified by the successful appeal in that case, *Fairford Water Ski Club Ltd v Cohoon* [2021] EWCA Civ 143; [2021] B.C.C. 498. First, it was clear on appeal that the question fell to be decided by reference to s.317 of the Companies Act 1985 rather than the provisions of the Companies Act 2006. The transaction in question was a management agreement entered between the company and a partnership of which the allegedly defaulting director was a partner. The directors of the company knew of the conflict (and were reminded of it at a board meeting) prior to the agreement being concluded, at a time when the negotiation of the fee was at large. They then knew that the company had not obtained any independent valuation in concluding an agreement with the partnership, with full knowledge of the director's interest in the partnership. It was not alleged that the director had breached any other duty, such as his duty to act in good faith in the best interests of the company. The Court of Appeal observed that it would be strange if the requirements of a specific declaration under s.317(1) of the Companies Act 1985 should be more onerous than those of a general notice under s.317(3) of that Act (cf. ss.177 and 185 of the 2006 Act). The Court of Appeal, at [31], per Males LJ, made the following observations as to the position under the 2006 Act:

> "31. For present purposes, three differences between the terms of s.317 of the 1985 Act and s.177 of the 2006 Act may be noticed: (1) The 1985 Act requires disclosure of 'the nature' of the director's interest in the contract, while the 2006 Act requires disclosure of "the nature and extent" of that interest; it was at one

> time suggested that this difference in language was significant, but the point fell away in the course of the hearing. (2) The 1985 Act requires disclosure at a meeting of the directors, but notice (other than a general notice) may also be given in other ways under the 2006 Act. (3) The 2006 Act contains express provision, which the 1985 Act does not, stating that disclosure is unnecessary if or to the extent that the other directors are already aware of the director's interest or reasonably ought to be."

EQUITY'S STRICTNESS

The strictness of the "no conflict" rule

To the end of the last paragraph, add:

In *Re Stratos Club* [2020] EWHC 3485 (Ch) at [292]–[297], it was held that where an opportunity is likely to be commercially attractive to the company, the director comes under a duty to bring it to the attention of the company, regardless of whether the company had the means to exploit the opportunity, applying *Bhullar v Bhullar* [2003] EWCA Civ 424; [2003] B.C.C. 711 and *Davies v Ford* [2020] EWHC 686 (Ch). **5-54**

After the first paragraph, add a new paragraph:

Re Allied Business & Financial Consultants Ltd [2009] EWCA Civ 751; [2009] B.C.C. 822 was applied in *Re Gallium Funds Solutions Ltd* [2021] EWHC 765 (Ch) at [66]–[68] and [164]–[165] and discussed and applied in *Re Capital Investment Centre Ltd* [2021] EW Misc 7 (CC), where it was held that the duty of the directors is to inform the company of an opportunity of which they become aware in their capacity as such, even if it is not within the scope of the business, even if the company does not have the resources to exploit it, even if the company has expressed a view that it does not want to take up further opportunities and even if the company is on the verge of being broken up or liquidated. See too *Re GO DPO EU Compliance Ltd* [2021] EWHC 1765 (Ch) at [147]–[148]. **5-56**

After the last paragraph, add a new paragraph:

Nevertheless, in *Parker v Auswild* [2022] VSCA 8, it was said:

> "where a reasonable person would think that there was a real or substantial possibility of a director being swayed by his or her personal interest, the director will breach the conflict rule, notwithstanding any relaxation of the conflict rule contemplated by *Streeter* [*Streeter v Western Areas Exploration (No.2)* [2011] WASCA 17] and *Mills* [*Mills v Mills* [1938] HCA 4; (1938) 60 C.L.R. 150]."

MODIFICATION/DILUTION OF THE "NO CONFLICT" RULE BY THE ARTICLES OF ASSOCIATION OR SHAREHOLDERS' AGREEMENT

The 2006 Act

Replace the first paragraph with:

Under the new statutory regime, the effect of the decision in *Movitex v Bulfield* (see para.5-63) has been expressly preserved: ss.180(4)(b) and 232(4) of the 2006 Act; EN 315–316, 319–320. However, it appears that the court has no discretion **5-66** to waive a technical irregularity: *Fairford Water Ski v Cohoon* [2020] EWHC 290 (Comm). On appeal, in *Fairford Water Ski Club Ltd v Cohoon* [2021] EWCA Civ 143; [2021] B.C.C. 498, it was found, however, that there was no breach and that the first instance judge had construed the relevant requirements as to declarations of conflict too stringently (in that case, those of the 1985 Act, whereas those of the 2006 Act are in certain respects yet less onerous); moreover, although the result made the point academic, it was suggested that there might be a compelling case for relief under s.1157 of the Companies Act 1985 as respects a putative breach of such a highly technical nature, as to which see para.5-71.

THE LEAVING DIRECTOR—DIRECTORSHIP WEAKENED OR TERMINATED

After the last paragraph, add a new paragraph:

5-69 In *Re Electrical Control Installations Ltd* [2021] EWHC 2661 (Ch); [2022] B.C.C. 199, applying *Foster Bryant Surveying v Bryant*, the Court found that there had been no breach by a director in setting up a competing business after his resignation, where there was no evidence that business opportunities had been diverted and the new business did not start to trade until after the resignation.

RELIEF BY THE COURT

After the second sentence in the first paragraph, add:

5-71 Cf., e.g. *Fairford Water Ski Club Ltd v Cohoon* [2021] EWCA Civ 143; [2021] B.C.C. 498 at [59], per Males LJ, obiter, as to the likelihood of the Court granting relief if the breach were of a highly technical nature.

PERSONAL CLAIM BY SHAREHOLDER AGAINST DIRECTORS

Common law

After the last paragraph, add a new paragraph:

5-74 A person may be liable in tort not as a primary tortfeasor but by accessory liability, a principle which applies, potentially, to directors, but gives rise to difficult questions in that context. In *Barclay-Watt v Alpha Panareti Public Ltd* [2022] EWCA Civ 1169, a property development company had been found to have been negligent as respects statements made in its marketing material which placed heavy emphasis on the availability of cheap mortgages in Swiss francs without referring to currency risks. The claimants also sued the managing director personally, who had undoubtedly been involved in the marketing strategy but had no direct contact with the purchasers. The Court of Appeal had no difficulty in upholding the judge's decision that the managing director was not a primary tortfeasor: he, himself, had assumed no responsibility to the claimants as distinct from that assumed by the company. But the question of when a director can become liable as an accessory was said to be elusive and fact-sensitive. The nature of the tort is important: thus, dicta in cases concerning, e.g. strict liability torts (of which *Fish & Fish Ltd v Sea Shepherd UK* [2015] UKSC 10; [2015] A.C. 1229 was an example), may not be directly applicable to a tort for which assumption of responsibility is a necessary element. It is a key principle that a company is a distinct legal entity, through which individuals may limit their liability. In the instant case, the managing director was not liable as an accessory: see [81]–[82], per Males LJ:

> "81. It can perhaps be said that there was a common design between APP [the company] and Mr Ioannou [the managing director] to market the properties in the way in which they were in fact marketed, and that this did not include any warning about the currency risks, but to hold that this amounts to a common design sufficient to incur personal liability as an accessory appears to lead to an unduly wide view of the personal liability of directors and senior managers in such cases. While the possibility of apportioning responsibility in contribution proceedings between the company on the one hand and directors and senior managers on the other goes some way to mitigate this difficulty, it is not a complete answer, not least if the company becomes insolvent. In that case, to impose liability on the directors and senior managers would be (as Lord Macnaghten put it in *Salomon v Salomon)* to expose them to 'the harsh provisions of the bankruptcy law'.
>
> 82. For these reasons I would hold, at the first stage [viz. not needing to go onto consider whether the director had done no more than 'exercise his constitutional role'] , that Mr Ioannou did not incur personal accessory liability in this case."

Fiduciary relationship between directors and shareholders

After the last paragraph, add a new paragraph:

In *Kelly v Baker* [2022] EWHC 1879 (Comm) at [17]–[35], there is a discussion of authorities as to circumstances in which a fiduciary relationship may arise (in the result, no such relationship arose). **5-77**

CHAPTER 6

The Derivative Claim

TABLE OF CONTENTS

THE RULE IN FOSS V HARBOTTLE AND THE "FRAUD ON THE MINORITY" EXCEPTION THERETO

The common law regime

Replace the second and third paragraphs (before the quote) with:

In *Prudential*, it was held that the rule would be subverted if a shareholder could recover damages for loss which was merely reflective of the loss suffered by the company: see paras 11-06–11-08 and the recent restatement of the rule by the Supreme Court in *Sevilleja v Marex Financial Ltd* [2020] UKSC 31; [2021] A.C. 309. It was further held that a claimant pursuing a derivative claim had at the outset to obtain the permission of the court to pursue it—by analogy now with an application under CPR 19.9: see para.6-14 and *Boston Trust Co Ltd v Verhoef* [2021] EWCA Civ 1176; [2022] B.C.C. 1. In *Barrett v Duckett*,[19] Peter Gibson LJ provided the following summary (at 249–250): 6-06

[19] *Barrett v Duckett* [1995] 1 B.C.L.C. 243 CA (Civ Div); see also *Nurcombe v Nurcombe* [1985] 1 W.L.R. 370 CA (Civ Div).

After the penultimate paragraph, add a new paragraph:

6-07 In *McGaughey v Universities Superannuation Scheme Ltd* [2022] EWHC 1233 (Ch); [2022] B.C.C. 982 at [43] applying *Harris v Microfusion*, Leech J held that

> "claimants in a common law derivative claim had to establish (1) they had sufficient interest or standing to pursue the claims on a derivative basis on behalf of a company or other entity; (2) a prima facie case that each individual claim fell within one of the established exceptions to the rule in *Foss v Harbottle 67 E.R. 189* (1843) 2 Hare 461, which prevented a member from bringing proceedings in their own name against the company; (3) a prima facie case on the merits in respect of each claim; and (4) it was appropriate in all the circumstances to permit them to pursue the derivative claim."

In order to establish that they had standing or a sufficient interest to continue the instant claim, it was essential for the claimants to demonstrate both that the company had suffered a loss and that loss was reflective of their own loss, for, if the shareholder had suffered non-reflective loss, then a personal claim would lie. The claimants relied in that case on the fourth exception to the rule in *Foss v Harbottle*, namely that a fraud had been committed and the members were prevented from remedying the fraud because the company was controlled by the wrongdoers. In relation to that exception, a derivative claimant had to establish a prima facie case that the defendants had committed a deliberate or dishonest breach of duty or that they had improperly benefitted themselves at the expense of the company (although the nature of that benefit need not be exclusively financial). A prima facie case on the merits was a higher test than a seriously arguable case and the court had to be satisfied that in the absence of an answer by the defendant the derivative claimant would be entitled to judgment. Where the facts were disputed, the court should find that a prima facie case had been made out only where there were issues of fact on which it would be wrong to accept the company's evidence without cross-examination. Contrast the more nuanced test as to the merits of a statutory derivative claim: *Re Nexbell Ltd* [2021] EWHC 1258 (Ch); [2021] B.C.C. 904 at [16]–[25], discussed in para.6-21. See also *Boston Trust Co Ltd v Verhoef* [2020] EWHC 1136 (Ch), where it was common ground that a prima facie case in a common law derivative claim was "roughly equivalent to showing a good or strong arguable case required in the context of jurisdictional gateways or freezing injunctions": [61]–[64]: *sed quaere*.

After the last paragraph, add a new paragraph:

In *Wang Pengying v Ng Wing Fai* [2021] HKCA 100; [2021] 1 HKLRD 997, the Hong Kong Court of Appeal (per Kwan V-P at [52]–[66] and Yuen JA at [79]–[90]) considered obiter that the true test as respects claims involving breach of duty which did not amount to actual fraud was the lawfulness of the majority (actually or probably) voting to exonerate the director(s) from breach, applying a proper purpose test to members' votes and that the test of "wrongdoer benefit" in *Harris v Microfusion 2003-2 LLP* [2016] EWCA Civ 1212; [2017] 1 B.C.L.C. 305 should not be adopted. Such a "proper purpose test" would require that members exercise their voting power bona fide for the purpose for which it was given; it would not be a proper exercise of the power to vote to achieve ends outside the scope of the 'social contract' between all shareholders (without any suggestion that shareholders owe a fiduciary duty to the company, nor of impugning their proprietary rights). Thus, it would be assumed that a director voting as a shareholder to exonerate himself from breach of duty would not be exercising his voting power for proper purposes and, depending on the facts, such an improper purpose might be ascribed to other shareholders.

THE NEW STATUTORY REGIME: PART 11 OF THE 2006 ACT

The cause of action that may be pursued as a derivative claim

After the second paragraph, add a new paragraph:

In *Hughes v Burley* [2021] EWHC 104 (Ch) at [108], it was held that a breach of a duty owed pursuant to a contract was a "breach of duty" for the purposes of the 2006 Act. **6-08**

Locus standi

After the penultimate paragraph, add new paragraphs:

In *Fruit Shippers Ltd v Petrie* [2020] NZHC 749, it was held that the sole effective beneficiary of a discretionary trust which held shares in the relevant company had standing to bring a common law (double) derivative claim, where the alleged wrongdoer was both a director and a trustee of the trust (and was in a position to block any board decision of the company and any decision for the trust). New Zealand has a statutory code for shareholder derivative claims (of wider application than the Companies Act 2006, so as to cover claims as respects related companies such that many forms of double/multiple derivative claims which would be governed by the common law in this jurisdiction fall within the statutory code in New Zealand). As here, the statutory code does not exclude a common law derivative claim and it was held that the jurisdiction should be exercised in a pragmatic and flexible way, and that the claimant had locus standi: "the common thread … is a willingness to allow standing to someone with sufficient interest if it is required to see that justice can be done." at [46], per Bell AJ. *Fruit Shippers Ltd v Petrie* was followed in *Singh v Auckland Taxi Service Ltd* [2021] NZHC 2157 so as to allow a derivative claim by a member of an industrial provident society (not being a shareholder within the statutory definition). **6-10**

In *Boston Trust Co Ltd v Verhoef* [2021] EWCA Civ 1176; [2022] B.C.C. 1, it was held that a judge should not have granted permission to continue a double derivative action conditional upon the success of an application to rectify a company's register in order to have standing. The claimants could establish neither a legal nor beneficial interest in the shares in question, and some form of equitable interest falling short of a full beneficial interest was not sufficient (see the first instance decision at [2020] EWHC 1136 (Ch) at [65]–[70] and [105]–[122], not challenged on appeal). After reference to *Re Starlight Developers Ltd* [2007] B.C.C. 929, it was said that the proper course would have been to stay the application, pending the outcome of the application to rectify the register (by the time, however, the appeal was heard, the register had been rectified and unconditional permission to continue the double derivative claim was granted).

Wrongdoer control

To the end of the first paragraph, add:

In *Prinse v Landmasters (Overseas) Ltd* [2022] EWHC 1921 (Ch), it was held that the common law test allowed, exceptionally, a derivative claim by a majority shareholder if there was some inhibition preventing exercise of majority control, but on the facts, the majority shareholder was not so inhibited. **6-11**

THE GRANT OR REFUSAL BY THE COURT OF PERMISSION TO CONTINUE THE DERIVATIVE CLAIM

The nature and purpose of the inter partes permission hearing

After the last paragraph, add a new paragraph:

6-15 See *Re Nexbell Ltd* [2021] EWHC 1258 (Ch); [2021] B.C.C. 904 at [5]–[29] for a recent distillation of the principles applicable to the issue of whether to grant permission to continue.

THRESHOLD CRITERIA

(1) The duty to promote the success of the company

To the end of the penultimate paragraph, add:

6-17 Cf. *Re Capital Investment Centre Ltd* [2021] EW Misc 7 (CC) at [56]–[57].

(2) Authorisation or ratification by the company—s.263(2)

Replace the paragraph with:

6-18 Section 263(2) of the 2006 Act provides that, if the act or omission of the director has been either authorised or ratified by the company in compliance with s.239, the court must refuse permission to continue with the action. But s.239(4), marking a significant break with the old law, provides that any resolution by members to ratify any breach of duty on the part of a director is only valid if taken without reliance upon the votes by the director or any connected person. See *Parry v Bartlett* [2012] B.C.C. 700; and paras 3-11 and 5-48.[44]

[44] See *Hook v Sumner* [2016] B.C.C. 220; *Brannigan v Style* [2016] EWHC 512 (Ch).

FACTORS GOING TO EXERCISE OF DISCRETION

The importance that a person acting in accordance with the director's general duty to promote the success of the company (s.172) would attach to continuing it: s.263(3)(b)

After the first paragraph, add a new paragraph:

6-21 See *Re Nexbell Ltd* [2021] EWHC 1258 (Ch); [2021] B.C.C. 904 at [16]–[25] for a review of the authorities as to this aspect starting with Lewison J's observation in *Iesini v Westrip Holdings* [2010] B.C.C. 420 at [79] to the effect that at the second stage something more than a prima facie case was needed and going on to the qualifications to that formulation expressed in *Stainer v Lee* [2010] EWHC 1539 (Ch); [2011] B.C.C. 134 at [29]; *Kleanthous v Paphitis* [2011] EWHC 2287 (Ch); [2012] B.C.C. 676 at [42]; *Abouraya v Sigmund* [2014] EWHC 277 (Ch); [2015] B.C.C. 503 at [53]; and *Saatchi v Gajjar* [2019] EWHC 3472 (Ch) at [29], concluding at [25] that

> "(1) The strength of the proposed claim is important. While there is no particular threshold test, at the very least a prima facie case (which if unanswered would entitle the company to judgment) is required. (2) The strength of the proposed claim is not, however, determinative—there are other (often quasi-commercial) factors to be taken into account too. These may include (but are not limited to) the size of the claim, the cost of bringing

the claim, the risk of adverse costs orders, and the prospects of recovery if successful. For example, a claim which is very strong on the merits but where there is virtually no prospect of recovery may well fail to cross the line; a case which is weaker but of huge financial or other significance, by contrast, may well in the balancing exercise be able to cross that line. (3) In carrying out the above exercise, the court should not embark on a mini-trial. Instead, it should form a view on the basis of the evidence before it at the hearing—which is likely to be more than the evidence which was before the court at the time of the first (on paper) stage consideration."

Whether the claimant has another remedy in his own right: s.263(3)(f)

The statutory oppression remedies

Replace the last sentence of the first paragraph with:

In some circumstances, an unfair prejudice petition may not be the appropriate remedy: see paras 6-42 and 7-60. **6-25**

After the penultimate paragraph, add a new paragraph:

In *Gill v Thind* [2020] EWHC 2973 (Ch) at [79]–[91], a derivative claim (alleging breach of directors' duty as respects payments by the company to a bank account from which the directors' children's school fees were paid, where it was disputed whether these had been authorised as dividends) was not permitted to continue as a matter of discretion, with reliance being placed on the existence of the unfair prejudice jurisdiction as an "eminently suitable" alternative remedy.

Other factors

Wrongdoer control and insolvency

Replace the third paragraph with:

A derivative claim may be brought even if the company is insolvent, where the cause of action was that the controlling directors had enriched themselves to the prejudice of other shareholders through a pre-pack administration and sale: *Montgold Capital LLP v Ilska* [2018] EWHC 2982 (Ch) (cf. *Hughes v Burley* [2021] EWHC 104 (Ch) in which the insolvency of the company was not a bar to a derivative claim, but the possibility that the company would remain insolvent even if the claim was successful was something which factored heavily in the exercise of the discretion to grant permission, particularly as to whether someone acting in accordance with the duty under s.172 would pursue the claim; in the event, permission was refused, a significant factor being that the claimant, while indicating that he would fund the claim, had offered no undertaking and no evidence of his means). In Australia, the position was summarised as follows: **6-29**

"7. There was no issue as to the standing of the plaintiff, as a shareholder, to make an application of this type. It is well established that creditors and members of a company have standing to seek leave to bring a derivative action in the name of a company in liquidation: *Chahwan v Euphoric Pty Ltd t/as Clay & Michael* [2008] NSWCA 52; (*Chahwan v Euphoric*) at [124], cited in the judgment of *Re DH International Pty Ltd (in liq) (sub nom Challis v Hoffman)* [2017] NSWSC 870 (*Challis v Hoffman*) at [5] per Gleeson JA.

8. The parties were also agreed as to the applicable principles in such an application. They were summarised by Barrett J in *Carpenter v Pioneer Park Pty Ltd* [2008] NSWSC 551; 71 NSWLR 577 (*Carpenter*) at [34], stating that the Court will have regard to 'three main matters':

(1) Whether the proceedings proposed to be pursued have some solid foundation, in

that they exhibit such a degree of merit as to be neither vexatious nor oppressive and to present reasonable prospects of success (Issue 1).

(2) The liquidator's attitude to the question whether the proceedings should be pursued (Issue 2).

(3) Whether practical considerations support the initiation of the proceedings, with particular reference to financial protection of the liquidator and the estate of the company by means of indemnity and, if indicated, security (Issue 3)."

(*Wu v Li* [2018] ACTSC 224.)

THE POWERS OF THE COURT

After the second paragraph, add a new paragraph:

6-31 In *Boston Trust Co Ltd v Verhoef* (Unreported 14 October 2022, Mr Ian Karet sitting as a Deputy High Court Judge), the defendants applied to terminate the orders made at earlier hearings (see *Boston Trust Co Ltd v Verhoef* [2020] EWHC 3042 (Ch) discussed under para.6-37) which had granted the claimants permission to bring the proceedings as derivative proceedings and a costs indemnity order. The defendants relied upon the fact that the claimants had over two years after the commencement of the derivative claim, and then only for limitation reasons, issued proceedings to enforce their claim to a 50% shareholding, whereas they had previously only mentioned such a claim as having a "theoretical existence". The learned Deputy Judge noted that he had jurisdiction to review the orders on the ground of a material change of circumstances but concluded that there had been no such material change. He accepted that this was a "partnership bust-up" (see *Mumbray v Lapper* [2005] EWHC 1152 (Ch); [2005] B.C.C. 990 at [25]), but concluded that it would have been possible from the outset to describe the case as such.

6-33 *Change title of section to:*

THE "DOUBLE/MULTIPLE-DERIVATIVE" CLAIM

After the first paragraph, add a new paragraph:

A "multiple-derivative claim" is one where there are several intermediate companies: see *Boston Trust Co Ltd v Verhoef* [2021] EWCA Civ 1176; [2022] B.C.C. 1 at [13] and *McGaughey v Universities Superannuation Scheme Ltd* [2022] EWHC 1233 (Ch); [2022] Bus. L.R. 797 at [17]–[22].

Replace the second paragraph with:

Such a "double/multiple-derivative" claim does not fall within the definition of a "derivative claim" within s.260(1) of the Act because the claimant is not a shareholder in the wronged company, but it can still be brought outside the new code under the previous and continuing common law regime: *Re Fort Gilkicker* [2013] Ch. 551.[53] Section 260(1) defines a "derivative claim" as one brought by "a member of a company (a) in respect of a cause of action vested in the company, and (b) seeking relief on behalf of the company". So, a "double-derivative" claim is not a "derivative claim" within that definition. Section 260(2) then goes on to provide that a "derivative claim" may only be brought under the Act or with the permission of the court under s.994. But s.260(2) does not preclude a derivative claim which falls outside the definition of a derivative claim in the Act, such as a "double-derivative" claim: *Re Fort Gilkicker* [2013] Ch. 551.[54]

[53] Contrast the position in the BVI by virtue of the different wording of its statutory code: *Novatrust Ltd v Kea Investments Ltd* [2014] EWHC 4061 (Ch) at [33].

[54] Briggs J, in reaching this conclusion, approved at [41] the view to that effect expressed in para.6-31 of the sixth edition of this work. In *Abouraya v Sigmund* [2015] B.C.C. 503, David Richards J expressly agreed with the reasoning and result in the *Re Fort Gilkicker* case. See also *Bhullar v Bhullar* [2016] B.C.C. 134; and *Harris v Microfusion* [2017] 1 B.C.L.C. 305, noted under para.6-07.

After the second paragraph, add a new paragraph:

In *Boston Trust Co Ltd v Verhoef* [2021] EWCA Civ 1176; [2022] B.C.C. 1, it was held that a double or multiple derivative claim required the permission of the court, but not as a result of CPR 19.9 which does not directly apply to a double or multiple derivative claim, but rather as a matter of court-developed practice and now operating by analogy with the rules for a statutory derivative claim.

PROCEDURE

Principle 12 (continued)

Replace item "(4)" with:

(4) The procedure for the bringing of a statutory derivative claim is now governed by CPR r.19.9–19.9F and Practice Direction 19C—Derivative Claims.

After the last paragraph, add a new paragraph:

In *Boston Trust Co Ltd v Verhoef* [2021] EWCA Civ 1176; [2022] B.C.C 1 it was held that CPR r.19.9 does not apply to double derivative claims (nor rr.19.9A, 19.9B) but there is a requirement for an *in limine* application to the court for permission to pursue a non-statutory derivative claim: see at [20], per David Richards LJ "the court is entitled and right to impose this requirement, and to apply by analogy the practice in CPR 19.9" which implies that the same procedure will be adopted as respects non-statutory derivative claims, viz. preliminary consideration on paper by way of filter, then determination of the application at a hearing on notice to the company and any other proper respondent.

Initial filter stage

After the last paragraph, add a new paragraph:

Quaere whether an application for permission can be made on notice to the respondents so as to bypass the ex parte stage? But the requirements in CPR r.19.9A appear mandatory at least as respects a statutory derivative claim: viz. that the company must not be made a respondent to the permission application but rather must be notified of it (subject to CPR r.19.9A(7)). See *McDonald v Horn* [1995] 1 All E.R. 961 CA (Civ Div), cited in para.6-38. **6-35**

WALLERSTEINER AND OTHER COSTS ORDERS

Replace the fourth paragraph with:

Boston Trust Co Ltd v Verhoef [2020] EWHC 3042 (Ch) at [26]–[35] contains a review of the authorities, from which the learned Deputy Judge held at [36] that the starting point was that a derivative claimant, having established that the proceedings are properly in the interests of the company by obtaining permission to continue, should be entitled to an indemnity. There was no requirement for a derivative claimant to show that an indemnity was needed on a "lack of funds basis" [49] (and a note in the then current *White Book* to CPR r.19.9E suggesting that an **6-37** indemnity will only lie if the applicants demonstrate it is genuinely needed, referring to *Smith v Croft (No.1)* [1986] 1 W.L.R. 580; [1986] 2 All E.R. 551, did not correctly state the law). *Sed quaere* whether this pays sufficient attention to the need for caution: see para.6-38. If the court is initially minded to grant a costs indemnity order, it will often make provision for its review by the court generally as the litigation progresses: *Re Wishart Petitioner* 2010 S.C. 16; *Fraser v Oystertec* [2005] B.P.I.R. 389, para.6-31.

CHAPTER 7

The Unfair Prejudice Remedy: Principles

TABLE OF CONTENTS

THE STATUTORY CONCEPT OF UNFAIRNESS

Lord Wilberforce leads the way

Replace the first sentence of the third paragraph with:

In reaching his conclusion, effectively overruling *Elder v Elder & Watson* 1952 S.C. 49 on this issue, Lord Wilberforce first dismissed any notion that the just and equitable remedy was limited to the protection of the minority's interests as a shareholder, as opposed to an employee or a director (at 374–375): 7-05

A broader interpretation of the unfair prejudice remedy

To the end of the second paragraph, after "446 at [6]–[17]", add:

7-14 ; *Siah v Wong* [2021] WASC 19 at [54]–[62].

After the last paragraph, add a new paragraph:

See *Financial Technology Ventures II (Q) LP v ETFS Capital Ltd* [2021] JCA 176 at [54]–[69] for the approach in Jersey as to art.141 Companies (Jersey) Law 1991 (having similar wording to s.994) derived in large part from English authority. The Court of Appeal there placed emphasis on the general wording of the legislation, holding at [69] and [72] that a finding of unfairness is not dependent on establishing either a breach of a legal right or duty or a breach of a legitimate expectation, in the sense of some agreement or understanding short of a binding contract, or of some quasi-partnership arrangement. On one interpretation of this decision, Jersey law may follow New Zealand law in playing down the insistence in *O'Neill v Phillips* that unfairness had to be found in settled and established equitable rules (if not in the formal constitution).

CONDUCT OF AFFAIRS OF THE COMPANY

An act or omission of the company or the conduct of the company's affairs

After the quote in the last paragraph, add new paragraphs:

7-21 In *Re Kings Solutions Ltd* [2021] EWCA Civ 1943; [2022] B.C.C. 529 at [54]–[61], following *Graham v Every* [2014] EWCA Civ 191; [2014] B.C.C. 376, it was held to be necessary to establish a causal connection between the actions complained of and the conduct of the companies' affairs. Thus, in *Graham v Every*, breach of a pre-emption agreement could not, of itself, amount to conduct of the company's affairs, but since the breach arguably had a direct impact on the way in which the parties had agreed the shareholders/directors were to be remunerated for their work in the company's business by way of dividend, there was a sufficient link to bring the complaint within the scope of "conduct of the company's affairs" for the purposes of s.994. By contrast, in *Re King's Solutions*, allegations of personal conduct such as the alleged obstruction by the majority shareholder of the exercise of a put option had no causal connection with conduct of the company's affairs (and no such connection was identified in the petition).

In *Re Cardiff City Football Club (Holdings) Ltd* [2022] EWHC 2023 (Ch), it was said that the majority shareholder (who was also a sizeable creditor) was entitled to exercise such commercial pressure as was at his disposal in his own interests, even if he was motivated by a personal feeling of vindictiveness towards a minority shareholder. His actions on his own account qua shareholder and creditor did not amount to conduct of the affairs of the company and there was no relevant allegation of breach of the articles, any shareholders' agreement or equitable constraints.

Associated companies

After the last paragraph, add a new paragraph:

7-22 In *Loveridge v Loveridge* [2020] EWCA Civ 1104 and *Loveridge v Loveridge* [2021] EWCA Civ 1697; [2022] B.C.C. 324, there were five companies and three partnerships capable of being characterised as one business. For the purpose of relief (and, therefore, interim relief), the distinct legal entities must be kept clearly in mind: [2020] EWCA Civ 1104 at [45]–[46]; in the second appeal [2021] EWCA Civ 1697 at [67], this was repeated but it was also said that the Court should not ignore the wider factual context and an overly strict approach should not be taken to the question of whether the petitioner has suffered a particular detriment as regards a particular company.

Other examples

After the last paragraph, add a new paragraph:

In *Lily Property Nominees Ltd v Stonebridge* [2020] EWHC 2113 (Ch), among a catalogue of complaints in relation to the affairs of an estate management company, many were found not to amount to conduct of the affairs of the company. An appeal, [2022] EWHC 76 (Ch), whose scope was limited to one complaint as respects criticism of the board as to their response to an incident in which the gardener was alleged to have been racist to the petitioners, was refused for a number of reasons, including that it was said to have nothing to do with protecting the petitioners' interests as shareholders from existing wrongs and as a matter of discretion no relief would have been appropriate even if the appeal had not been unsuccessful for other reasons. **7-24**

INTERESTS AS A SHAREHOLDER

Broad interpretation

After the last paragraph, add new paragraphs:

Cf. *Loveridge v Loveridge* [2021] EWCA Civ 1697; [2022] B.C.C. 324 at [67]–[70] endorsing the broad approach as to interests as a shareholder, but also endorsing *Re JE Cade & Son* [1991] B.C.C. 360; [1992] B.C.L.C. 213: **7-26**

> "I would respectfully agree with the comment expressed by Warner J in *Re JE Cade & Son Ltd* [1992] B.C.L.C. 213 at p.233 that what Lord Wilberforce [in *Ebrahimi v Westbourne Galleries* [1973] A.C. 360 at 374-375] was referring to was capacity in the strict sense, rather than suggesting that a shareholder could seek winding up on the just and equitable ground to protect a wider range of interests than could be protected by an unfair prejudice petition."

In *Albion Energy Ltd v Energy Investments Global BRL* [2020] EWHC 301 (Comm); [2020] 1 Lloyd's Rep. 501 at [75] a claim that a shareholder overpaid for the acquisition of shares was held not to be conduct prejudicial to its interests as a shareholder.

PREJUDICE

After the quote in the last paragraph, add a new paragraph:

In *Re Macom GmBH (UK) Ltd* [2021] EWHC 1661 (Ch) at [47]–[49], it was observed that prejudice need not be an actual or anticipated diminution of the value of shareholding. David Richards J in *Re Coroin* [2012] EWHC 2343 (Ch) was not ruling out a finding of unfair prejudice where acts have no financial consequence, merely rather saying that it may be more difficult to establish prejudice in such a case. **7-28**

Examples

After the sixth paragraph, add new a paragraph:

7-29 In *Financial Technology Ventures II (Q) LP v ETFS Capital Ltd* [2021] JCA 176 at [58(c)], the Jersey Court of Appeal commented upon the above passage as follows:

> "As a matter of principle, we would accept that a justifiable loss of confidence in the probity of a company's management is capable of constituting prejudice. However, even that statement needs to be understood in the relevant jurisprudential context. The concept of a 'justifiable loss of confidence in management' derives from the case-law on just and equitable winding-up, which is discussed in §271–272 below. In that context, it is not sufficient for a shareholder simply to assert that he disagrees with the commercial judgment of the controlling director/s. In order to establish a sufficiently justifiable loss of confidence in the probity of management, a shareholder has to establish some sufficiently relevant and serious breach of duty or breach of ordinary standards of business fair dealing on the part of management. This is illustrated by the authorities on which the proposition in Hollington is based. *Re Elgindata (No 1)* [1991] BCLC 959 was a case concerning breach of duty which involved a misapplication of company assets. *Re Edwardian Group Ltd* [2018] EWHC 1715 (Ch) also involved substantial breaches of fiduciary duty, the effect of which was to deprive shareholders of important information to which they were entitled and to cover up wrongdoing by the management. It was in those circumstances that the court found in each case that there was prejudice. Neither decision purports to lay down any generally applicable proposition of law to the effect that a justifiable loss of confidence in management will necessarily and of itself always constitute prejudice. Nor do we consider that any such general proposition could logically be sustained. If, for example, there has been a justifiable loss of confidence in management because there have been serious breaches of fiduciary duty, then that may well be a reason for regarding it as prejudicial, but the answer to the question will always be context specific and it will almost invariably depend upon a combination of factors (e.g. the cumulative effect of there having been a breach of duty, together with the financial impact on the company or the shareholders of that breach, and the resultant loss of confidence in management)."

After the seventh paragraph, add a new paragraph:

In *Re Macom GmBH (UK) Ltd* [2021] EWHC 1661 (Ch) at [47]–[49], the Court considered that the reasoning underlying *Re Baumler (UK) Ltd* [2005] B.C.C. 181 applies equally to a situation where the relationship was governed by a shareholders' agreement, particularly one with an obligation of good faith: the shareholders are entitled to expect adherence to those obligations and a failure to so adhere may amount to unfair prejudice even in the absence of financial loss. It also considered that the finding of unfair prejudice in *Re Edwardian Group Ltd* [2018] EWHC 1715 (Ch) in the corrosion of good administration and trust between shareholders and directors was not dependent on establishing financial loss (even though the petitioners in that case had been able to identify loss, in the loss of dividend income). In the instant case, the Court found unfair prejudice in the compromising of the good and proper administration and corporate governance of the company and the relationship between the parties under the shareholders' agreement.

BREACH OF AGREEMENTS/UNDERSTANDINGS AND OBLIGATIONS OF GOOD FAITH BETWEEN SHAREHOLDERS

Public-listed companies

After the last paragraph, add a new paragraph:

In *Re Klimvest Plc* [2022] EWHC 596 (Ch); [2022] B.C.C. 747 at [260]–[269], the Court addressed but did not decide the question of whether equitable constraints could exist between shareholders in a public listed company (and whether *Re Astec (BSR)* [1998] 2 B.C.L.C. 556 was correctly decided) in the context of a just-and-equitable winding-up petition alleging exclusion from management. HHJ Cawson QC, sitting as a Judge of the High Court, gave the obiter view at [269]: 7-32

> "I would venture to suggest that on appropriate facts, equitable considerations might arise as between shareholders in a public listed company, but that this would be a rare event given that the parties would, in almost all cases, have submitted themselves to acting on a purely commercial footing."

BREACH OF CONTRACT

Term of shareholders' agreement

Contractual duties of good faith

Replace the paragraph with:

These are discussed in paras 4-36–4-39. The parties may provide expressly for a contractual duty of good faith, even in companies which are otherwise purely commercial, arm's length relationships having none of the other usual hallmarks of quasi-partnerships: *McKillen v Barclay* [2012] EWHC 521 (Ch) (Richards J, interlocutory ruling); *Re Coroin Ltd* [2012] EWHC 2343 (Ch) (Richards J, trial); [2014] B.C.C 14 (appeal dismissed); *Re Compound Photonics Group Ltd* [2022] EWCA Civ 1371, reversing [2021] EWHC 787 (Ch) (Adam Johnson J). There is a growing body of authority that a duty of good faith may be implied in some long-term relational contracts such as quasi-partnerships: see para.4-37. 7-35

QUASI-PARTNERSHIPS AND COMMON UNDERSTANDINGS—APPLYING TRADITIONAL EQUITABLE PRINCIPLES—AND BORROWING FROM PARTNERSHIP LAW

"Quasi-partnership"

General

Replace footnote 66 with:

[66] See *Fisher v Cadman* [2006] 1 B.C.L.C. 499 at [84]; *Brett v Migration Solutions Holdings Ltd* [2016] EWHC 523 (Ch) at [193(i)]; *Waldron v Waldron* [2019] EWHC 115 (Ch); [2019] B.C.C. 682 at [27]. See also *Financial Technology Ventures II (Q) LP v ETFS Capital Ltd* [2021] JCA 176 at [63]–[69]. 7-40

After the last paragraph, add new paragraphs:

In *Chu v Lau* [2020] UKPC 24; [2020] 1 W.L.R. 4656 at [31], Lord Briggs emphasised that none of the three indicia of a quasi-partnership referred to by Lord Wilberforce in *Ebrahimi* at 379F–G (cited at para.7-05) represent necessary elements, in the sense that the absence of one or more is fatal to the establishment of a quasi-partnership (cf., similarly, per Lady Arden at [81], [83]). Thus, in that case, the absence of a restriction on the transfer of shares was in no way a sufficient basis to interfere with the trial judge's finding that the company was a quasi-partnership.

The successive appeals in *Loveridge v Loveridge* [2020] EWCA Civ 1104 and [2021] EWCA Civ 1697; [2022] B.C.C. 324 provide an illustration of where the boundaries of the concept of quasi-partnership may lie (and the need to articulate properly the basis for an assertion that a quasi-partnership exists) since in the first appeal, the assertion of equitable constraints was found to be unarguable, but in the second appeal, with the petition having been amended, the contrary was held. The case concerned three partnerships and five companies, all owned by various members of the Loveridge family and all conducting aspects of a caravan park business. The proportion of shareholdings in the company were not, however, uniform and not all relevant members of the family were directors of every company. By a proposed amendment to the petition at the first appeal, it was alleged that there were equitable constraints including a right to be involved in management on the part of the petitioner, but the allegations said to give rise to these were characterised as no more than an assertion that the petitioner had been the driving force behind the expansion of the companies and that he had run the companies on a day-to-day basis. Thus, Floyd LJ, with Lewison and Asplin LJJ agreeing, concluded ([2020] EWCA Civ 1104 at [52]) "Accordingly, I would hold that it was not open to the judge to find an arguable case of the equitable restraint on the companies' powers ...". The second appeal was against a refusal to strike out the petition in a further amended form. Falk J (with whom Nugee and Bean LJJ agreed) held at [2021] EWCA Civ 1697; [2022] B.C.C. 324 [71]–[74] that the further amendments in the petition did give rise to an arguable case of exclusion in breach of equitable constraints as to participation in management (as respects three of the companies but, in the event, the petition was struck out in its entirety for other reasons):

> "71. In my view, whilst still lacking in clarity, the amended petition does include sufficient new material to amount to an arguable claim that Michael has or had an entitlement to participate in the management of Kingsford, Riverside Stourport and Sales, such that (subject to the effect of the Court of Appeal's earlier decision) his exclusion from management could potentially justify a claim for relief. The position in relation to *Quatford* and *Breton Park* is considered separately below.
>
> 72. The basis for Michael's arguable entitlement arises from the pleaded history of Michael's association with his parents in what became known as the Riverside partnership. He traded with them in partnership from 1990, with each having a one third share. Profits were reinvested. Kingsford was only acquired in corporate form in 2004 because that was what was on offer, and it was held in the same shares as the partnership and with the same directors. Sales took over the partnership's caravan sales business in 2010 and was again held in the same shares and with the same directors. Its business was clearly related to that of the partnership because it handled sales of caravans on partnership sites. Riverside Stourport is a more recent acquisition but again is held in the same shares as the Riverside partnership and with the same directors.
>
> 73. This history, together with the close family links, provides a basis for asserting that, as with the partnership that actually existed, the association between

Michael, Ivy and Alldey was a personal relationship involving mutual confidence, in which there was an entitlement to participate in management. It would have been inherent in the terms of the Riverside partnership that Michael was entitled to participate in management (*Lindley & Banks on Partnership*, 20th ed. at 15-01; s 24(5) Partnership Act 1890). In this case this was reinforced by the actual conduct of the affairs of the partnership. It is arguable that Michael relied on an understanding of his entitlement to participate in continuing to work in the business and in allowing profits to be reinvested.

74. In *Westbourne Galleries* at pp.379-380 Lord Wilberforce recognised that the conversion of a pre-existing partnership into a limited company (as occurred on the facts of that case) was a common example of a situation where an association on the basis of a personal relationship involving mutual confidence would be found to exist, justifying the superimposition of equitable considerations on the legal structure of the company and its articles of association. The label quasi-partnership reflected the application, in that case through the remedy of winding up on just and equitable grounds, of principles that allowed the court to dissolve a partnership where there had been an exclusion from management, on the basis that such exclusion was contrary to the obligations owed between the partners."

Written shareholder agreements

Replace the second paragraph with:

Where the parties have entered into a detailed written agreement, the existence of such an agreement does not necessarily exclude equitable or fiduciary constraints but the terms of that agreement will be of primary importance in determining the rights, expectations and duties of the parties: see para.4-48, including the influential Australian authority, *United Dominion Corp v Brian Pty* (1985) 60 A.L.R 741 at 747 and *Hospital Products Ltd v United States Surgical Corp* (1984) 156 C.L.R. 41 at 97; see also *Re Company (No.002015 of 1996)* [1997] 2 B.C.L.C. 1 Ch D; *Ross River Ltd v Cambridge Football Club Ltd* [2007] EWHC 2115 (Ch) at [196]–[197]; *Re Audas Group Ltd* [2019] EWHC 2304 (Ch), where it was held at [134]–[140] that a shareholders agreement did not supersede the quasi-partnership understandings upon which the company had been established; *Re International Automotive Engineering Projects Ltd* [2022] EWHC 1751 (Ch) at [155]–[163] where the company was found to be a quasi-partnership, with the indicia thereof to be found in the express terms (particularly, an obligation of good faith between the shareholders and each shareholder having an entitlement to be a director); see also *Shrimpton v Scriven* 2 June 2016 Claim No.BVI HC (Com) 2014/0171 per Mr Sher QC AJ. See also *Re Compound Photonics Group Ltd* [2022] EWCA Civ 1371, reversing [2021] EWHC 787 (Ch) (Adam Johnson J), discussed in para.4-39. **7-41**

Entire agreement clauses

To the end of the first paragraph, add:

Cf. *Starling v The Climbing Gym Ltd* [2020] EWHC 1833 (Ch) at [95]–[97]. **7-42**

After the last paragraph, add new paragraphs:

In *Re A.B. Produce Trading Ltd* [2022] EWHC 1028 (Ch) at [359], the existence of a "no partnership" clause in an investment agreement entered into when three individuals acquired shares in a family quasi-partnership did not exclude the possibility that the company remained a quasi-partnership (and, on the facts, the original quasi-partners did remain subject to the same equitable restraints).

In *Re International Automotive Engineering Projects Ltd* [2022] EWHC 1751 (Ch), the company was found to be a quasi-partnership notwithstanding that there was a "whole agreement" clause and a "no partnership" clause in the shareholders' agreement. Mr Recorder Jack sitting as a Judge of the High Court emphasised that a company which is a quasi-partnership is not in law a partnership, so that a term which states that the shareholders were not in partnership does not prevent a company from being a quasi-partnership, commenting further that

> "the expression quasi-partnership is more of a metaphor: the company is not a partnership but the relations between those interested in the company are more akin to those of partners".

All of the indicia of a quasi-partnership were said to be reflected in the express terms of the shareholders' agreement, which included an obligation of good faith between the shareholders and each shareholder being entitled to be a director. See also *Re Compound Photonics Group Ltd* [2022] EWCA Civ 1371, reversing [2021] EWHC 787 (Ch) (Adam Johnson J), discussed in para.4-39.

Existence of quasi-partnership/enforceability in equity of understandings

After the quote in the fourth paragraph, add new paragraphs:

7-43 In *Ma Wai Fong v Kie Yik* [2022] UKPC 14; [2022] B.C.C. 953, it was said that while the head of a family might set up a family business in the hope or expectation that it would provide work and income to family members, that did not give rise to an entitlement that on the part of any particular family member to participate in management or to have a right of veto on decisions.

In *Re Derbyshire Aggregates Ltd* [2021] EWHC 2455 (Ch) at [45] the point was made that a company might be properly characterised as a quasi-partnership even though it had become large and successful: if it remains run relatively informally on the basis of consensus and trust and confidence, its size is not sufficient to bring to an end the equitable considerations which bind its owners.

Smith v Smith [2022] EWHC 1035 (Ch) at [99]–[127] contains a review of the main authorities as to the question of whether a company is a quasi-partnership (or subject to equitable constraints preventing exclusion from management).

Understandings between a section of shareholders

In the first paragraph, replace "Re Edwardian Group Ltd [2018] EWHC 1715 (Ch)" with:

7-45 *Re Edwardian Group Ltd* [2018] EWHC 1715 (Ch); [2019] 1 B.C.L.C. 171,

After the last paragraph, add new paragraphs:

In *Re Derbyshire Aggregates Ltd* [2021] EWHC 2455 (Ch) at [44], it was observed that the interposition of directors who are not shareholders does not mean that a company cannot remain a quasi-partnership: such a person may appreciate and adhere to the personal understanding between the other directors and respect it, subject to compliance with the statutory duties that all directors have.

In *Re A.B. Produce Trading Ltd* [2022] EWHC 1028 (Ch) at [346]–[360], the introduction of three new outside shareholders to a "family company" quasi-partnership was held not to affect the continuing existence of equitable constraints as between the "family" shareholders (not, however, binding on the new shareholders) where the size of the new shareholdings was very small as compared to the "family" shareholders, the new shareholders were all long-standing friends and/or advisers of the family, and notwithstanding that family members no longer had control of the board. At a later stage, however, the equitable constraint requiring the family shareholders to support the respective entitlement of each to participate in management, lapsed as respects the petitioner's participation, because he had substantially abdicated from such participation. The court expressed some preference for the view in *Waldron v Waldron* [2019] EWHC 115 (Ch); [2019] B.C.C. 682 that Fancourt J's observation at [134] in *Re Edwardian Group Ltd* [2018] EWHC 1715 (Ch); [2019] 1 B.C.L.C. 171 ("I am very doubtful whether the Petitioners are right in their argument [that a quasi-partnership can exist where only some shareholders are said to be within the scope of the management participation understanding], except perhaps in a case where the shareholders that are not parties to the equitable considerations are either a very small minority or are closely connected to the quasi-partners (as in *Fisher v Cadman*), such that the established quasi-partnership character of the company does not change") was overly restrictive. The equitable constraints between the "family" shareholders also survived a corporate restructuring, whereby the original company became a subsidiary of newly incorporated company of which the shareholdings reflected the original company.

In *Smith v Smith* [2022] EWHC 1035 (Ch), the company was found to be a quasi-partnership, it being said to be a case similar to *Fisher v Cadman* [2005] EWHC 377 (Ch); [2006] 1 B.C.L.C. 499 and *Waldron v Waldron* [2019] EWHC 115 (Ch); [2019] B.C.C. 682 where shares, in what was a quasi-partnership, have been transferred to the next generation, with the company remaining of the same essential character.

Changing relationships

After the second paragraph, add a new paragraph:

In *Re A.B. Produce Trading Ltd* [2022] EWHC 1028 (Ch), a family company which commenced as a quasi-partnership in which all shareholders did not cease to be such when two of the family shareholder directors resigned and two outside non-shareholder directors were appointed; nor did the equitable constraints between the quasi-partners cease when three other parties acquired modest shareholdings, although those new shareholders were held not to be subject to these. **7-48**

A duty of good faith

To the end of the first paragraph, add:

For cases where the petitioners relied upon a breach of an express duty of care in a shareholders' agreement, see *Re Compound Photonics Group Ltd* [2022] EWCA Civ 1371, reversing [2021] EWHC 787 (Ch) (Adam Johnson J), discussed in para.4-39. **7-51**

Breach of duty of good faith

To the end of the first paragraph, add:

In *Re Compound Photonics Group Ltd* [2022] EWCA Civ 1371, reversing [2021] EWHC 787 (Ch) (Adam Johnson J), it was held that the minority shareholders had not been unfairly prejudiced by the conduct of the affairs of the company by the majority, and in particular the exclusion of certain directors from management, because the terms of its constitution, which included an express duty of good faith, did not entrench those directors in management: see para.4-39. **7-53**

To the end of the third paragraph, add:

Cf. *Re Cintep Development Ltd* [2020] EWHC 3210 (Ch), the majority breached, among other obligations, the obligation of good faith inherent in a quasi-partnership, in "killing off" the project, by, among other things, withdrawing funding.

BREAKDOWN OF TRUST AND CONFIDENCE

To the end of the first paragraph, before the full stop, add:

7-54 (cf. *Loveridge v Loveridge* [2021] EWCA Civ 1697; [2022] B.C.C. 324 at [114]–[117])

After the quote in the last paragraph, add a new paragraph:

7-56 *Shehata v Mansfield Hotel Ltd* [2021] EWHC 630 (Ch) is an example of where a quasi-partner could not complain of exclusion from management where he had '*self-excluded*'.

BREACH OF FIDUCIARY AND OTHER DUTIES BY DIRECTORS

After the first paragraph, add a new paragraph:

7-59 In *Re Rhys Williams (Bangor) Ltd* [2020] EWHC 2624 (Ch) at [82], it was held:

> "However, wrongful conduct by directors in a quasi-partnership will not be 'unfairly' prejudicial if the other quasi-partners have behaved in the same way on the understanding that there will later be a process of accounting and equalisation (for example, *Re Jayflex Construction Ltd* [2003] EWHC 2008 (Ch); [2004] B.C.L.C. 145)."

In the *Rhys Williams* case, three brothers who were quasi-partners in a farming business had reached the view that the business should be split. Two of the brothers transferred two pieces of farming land to a new company without the knowledge of the third. This was held to be plainly in breach of their duties as directors and unfairly prejudicial, despite protestations that it was to implement the anticipated 'demerger'. But a transfer of cash from the company to the new company was not treated as unfairly prejudicial: the third brother had known of this shortly after it happened and had not complained: no order would be made for repayment, but the monies would fall to be accounted for as used for the personal benefit of the two brothers.

RELATIONSHIP WITH THE DERIVATIVE CLAIM

Replace the penultimate paragraph with:

7-60 In *Re Hut Group Ltd* [2020] EWHC 5 (Ch), the court declined to strike out a petition based on breaches of duty by the directors, and also the relief claimed by way of an order for payment of equitable compensation to the company and the petitioner personally. On appeal see *Re The Hut Group Ltd* [2021] EWCA Civ 904; [2021] B.C.C. 970: although the point was not pursued on appeal that the petition should be struck out as being more appropriately a derivative claim, the Court of Appeal endorsed the first instance judge's analysis on this point at [44]–[45]. The key point in that case was that the petition did not allege that the company, as opposed to the petitioner, had suffered loss. The relationship between derivative claims and unfair prejudice claims are in general "highly sensitive to the precise circumstances of the case and the relief claimed." [45], per David Richards LJ. See also paras 6-25 and 6-42.

After the penultimate paragraph, add new paragraphs:

See too *Liu Tieh Ching Brandon v Liu Ju Ching* [2021] HKCFI 823; [2021] HKEC 1227 at [25]–[33] where an argument that an unfair prejudice petition should be struck out because the allegations should be determined by derivative claim was rejected: the allegations which the petitioner raised went to the establishing of unfairly prejudicial conduct and the context in which the petitioner claimed to be excluded; the petitioner did not seek any order for payment by the respondents to the company.

The scope of relief properly to be sought in an unfair prejudice petition arose indirectly in *Taylor Goodchild Ltd v Taylor* [2021] EWCA Civ 1135; [2022] 2 B.C.L.C. 27 in the context of whether a claim against a director and the company to which he had diverted profits was an abuse of process given an earlier s.994 petition which had resulted in the director being ordered to sell his shares. The Court of Appeal recognized that such relief—i.e. a claim against a director and a third party arising from the director's breach of duty—could be brought within a s.994 petition, but equally it was not a straightforward question as to whether it should be so brought, referring to *Re Chime Corp Ltd* [2004] 7 HKCFAR 546 and *Waddington Ltd v Chan Chun Hoo Thomas* [2009] 2 B.C.L.C. 82 which impacted on the question of whether the later claim was a *Henderson v Henderson* type abuse (and, in the result, it was held not to be).

APPLICATIONS OF THE UNFAIR PREJUDICE TEST

Exclusion from management

To the end of the first paragraph, add:

In *Chu v Lau* [2020] UKPC 24; [2020] 1 W.L.R. 4656 at [85], Lady Arden indicated that breach of an equitable entitlement to participation in management may be found notwithstanding that the quasi-partner remains a de jure director, if it has been made effectively impossible in some other way for him to participate in the management of the business. So too in *Martin v Hughes* [2021] CSOH 109 at [50], the Outer House observed that decisions taken in secret, or without informing, a quasi-partner could amount to a breach of an equitable constraint as respects management participation; and, if the matter was sufficiently momentous, even where the quasi-partner in question was no longer involved in day-to-day management. 7-63

After the second paragraph, add a new paragraph:

In *Re Compound Photonics Group Ltd* [2022] EWCA Civ 1371, reversing [2021] EWHC 787 (Ch) (Adam Johnson J), it was held that the minority shareholders had not been unfairly prejudiced by the conduct of the affairs of the company by the majority, and in particular the exclusion of certain directors from management, because the terms of its constitution, which included an express duty of good faith, did not entrench those directors in management: see para.4-39.

Justification for exclusion

After the fourth paragraph, add a new paragraph:

7-64 In *Starling v Climbing Gym Ltd* [2020] EWHC 1833 (Ch), the Petitioner was unsuccessful in establishing a quasi-partnership, but it was further held that his exclusion from management was in any event justified, due principally to his breach of s.175 of the Companies Act 2006 and misleading a disciplinary hearing.

Excessive remuneration and inadequate dividends

Excessive remuneration

After the last paragraph, add a new paragraph:

7-69 In *Re Stratos Club Ltd* [2020] EWHC 3485 (Ch) at [125]–[135], it was held that a salary of £350,000 was excessive on the basis of expert evidence, which indicated that £202,500 was reasonable, and it was unreasonable for the director to draw more than 50% of that after his responsibilities were split between two companies.

Inadequate dividends

After the last paragraph, add a new paragraph:

7-71 In *Re Derbyshire Aggregates Ltd* [2021] EWHC 2455 (Ch), the court was satisfied that a director/shareholder ensured that the company did not pay a sizeable dividend in order to apply pressure on his fellow shareholders in negotiations for the sale of his shares, breaching his duty to act in good faith and for proper purposes, and thus unfairly prejudicing them.

Loss of confidence in management

To the end of the first paragraph, add:

7-72 In *Re Compound Photonics Group Ltd* [2022] EWCA Civ 1371, reversing [2021] EWHC 787 (Ch) (Adam Johnson J), it was held that the minority shareholders had not been unfairly prejudiced by the conduct of the affairs of the company by the majority, and in particular the exclusion of certain directors from management, because the terms of its constitution, which included an express duty of good faith, did not entrench those directors in management: see para.4-39.

After the last paragraph, add a new paragraph:

In *Birchfield v Birchfield Holdings Ltd* [2021] NZCA 428, it was held at [59]–[60] that relief under the unfair prejudice jurisdiction is not available "in respect of: (a) differences about the appropriateness of business strategies arrived at in good faith by a company, or alleged errors of judgment by management, inefficiencies, or poor business management; and (b) disagreements over company strategy or management, or situations where minority shareholders differ from the majority on the policy and direction of a company which they see as being to their disadvantage".

Procedural irregularity

After the last paragraph, add a new paragraph:

7-73 In *Ming Siu Hung v JF Ming Inc* [2021] UKPC 1; [2021] B.C.C. 498, the Privy Council restored a share purchase order which had been made at first instance and overturned on appeal, which was based on a breach of a provision in the articles requiring a profit and loss account and balance sheet for the company together with majority shareholders passing of resolutions to remove that right as a response to the minorities seeking to enforce it. The Board commented at [32] that it shared the judge's view that the

> "refusal to provide financial information was in reality a symptom, albeit a very serious and harmful one, of his complete and continuing inability to recognise or acknowledge that the appellants had any legitimate stake in the Company as minority shareholders."

Share issues

After the last paragraph, add a new paragraph:

In *Re The Hut Group Ltd* [2021] EWCA Civ 904; [2021] B.C.C. 970, a central allegation was that the petitioners had been unfairly prejudiced by the dilution of their shareholding through successive rights issues. This aspect of the petition was struck out on the basis that the petition did not articulate particulars sufficient to support an allegation that the directors had acted in bad faith or for an improper purpose and, indeed, made no challenge to the commercial legitimacy of the share issues or the choice of allottees. **7-76**

The analogy of contractual frustration

After the last paragraph, add new paragraphs:

In *Re Lloyds Autobody Ringway Ltd* [2018] EWHC 2336 (Ch), HHJ Hodge QC held at [111]: **7-79**

> "I am satisfied that an objective and informed observer would fairly conclude that Mr Lynch-Smith's failure to buy out Mr Davies's 25% shareholding on a fair basis after he had terminated Mr Davies's management role and employment with the company was outside the parties' reasonable contemplation at the time when Ringway was established."

In *Smith v Smith* [2022] EWHC 1035 (Ch), where the petitioner was excluded from management by the majority exercising its power of removal under s.168 of the Companies Act 2006 (and he was dismissed from employment), the company was found to be a quasi-partnership and the exclusion was unfairly prejudicial conduct. HHJ Mark Cawson QC (sitting as a Judge of the High Court) went on, however, to say that, even if the company had not been a quasi-partnership (and the shareholders had not been subject to equitable constraints), he would still have found the petitioner's removal as a director (and dismissal from employment) without an offer to buy his shares to be unfairly prejudicial conduct:

> "126. ... In [*Re Lloyds Autobody Ringway Ltd*], HHJ Hodge QC, applying the final paragraph from the citation from the speech of Lord Hoffmann in *O'Neill v Phillips* [at 1101H–1102A], held that the petitioner, who was 25% shareholder, was entitled to an order pursuant to Section 996 of the 2006 Act that he be bought out notwithstanding that the company in question was not a quasi-partnership company, and the respondent 75% shareholder had grounds for removing the petitioner as an employee.
>
> 140. ... I would add that even if it had not been established that the Company was a quasi- partnership, or that Joan was subject to equitable constraints, I would have been prepared to find that, in the present circumstances, causing the Company to dismiss Tim, and then removing Tim as a director, without offering to purchase his shares at a fair value amounted to unfairly prejudicial conduct having regard to the considerations referred by Lord Hoffmann in *O'Neill v Phillips* at 1102H as applied by HHJ Hodge QC in *Re [Lloyds] Autobody Ringway Ltd* (supra) as applied to the facts of the present case."

ARBITRATION CLAUSES

After the first paragraph, add a new paragraph:

7-83 In *Caldicott Worldwide Ltd BVIHCM 2019/190* (13 October 2020), the relevant articles contained a clause which required "any difference between the Company ... and the members ... touching any breach or otherwise relating to any affairs of the Company" to be referred to arbitration. The minority shareholders complained of unfair prejudice in that dividends which had been declared were withheld from them (in contrast to other shareholders) and with the majority having wrongly purported to ratify this at a general meeting. A stay for arbitration was ordered as respects claims against the company, but the unfair prejudice proceedings, which included relief such as a buy-out order, were allowed to proceed as between the members (with the company remaining a party at least for the time being, having regard to e.g. the potential need for disclosure from it).

"CLEAN HANDS" AND MISCONDUCT ON THE PART OF THE PETITIONER

Replace footnote 130 with:

7-84 [130] See also, e.g. *Sang Lee Investment Co Ltd v Wing Kwai Investment Co Ltd* (1983) 127 Sol. Jo. 410; *Barrett v Duckett* [1995] B.C.C. 362 Ch D (Companies Ct); *Re Last Lion Holdings Ltd* [2018] EWHC 2347 (Ch) at [168]–[171]; *Chung-Yi v Chang* [2018] NSWSC 1112 at [75]. *Re Simply Alarming Security Ltd* [2020] EWHC 2263 (Ch) at [16].

DELAY AND ACQUIESCENCE

After the sixth paragraph, add new paragraphs:

7-87 In *Re International Automotive Engineering Projects Ltd* [2022] EWHC 1751 (Ch), the Court considered whether delay precluded allegations of unfair prejudice arising from breaches of directors' duty where there might be a limitation defence, but considered that the breaches, characterised as a failure to account for profits, were ongoing.

In *Hiscock v Penmure Orchards Ltd* [2021] NZHC 3020 (following *Alligators Fast Food Ltd v Chen* [2018] NZHC 587), it was held that no limitation period applied to the New Zealand unfair prejudice remedy, citing the jurisprudence of this jurisdiction, *Re Grandactual Ltd* [2005] EWHC 1415 (Ch); [2006] B.C.C. 73 and *Routledge v Skerritt* [2019] EWHC 573 (Ch); [2019] B.C.C. 812: rather delay factored into the question of discretion and it was unclear at the stage of an application for summary judgment whether the relevant complaint (treatment of remuneration over a long period) could be rightly characterised as a course of conduct starting in the remote past and continuing to the time of issue of proceedings.

Sumitomo Mitsuitrust UK Ltd et al v Spectrum Galaxy Ltd (unreported 14/4/21) BVIHC(COM) 2018/0172 is an example where the Court, having cited *Re Edwardian Group Ltd* [2018] EWHC 1715 (Ch); [2019] 1 B.C.L.C. 171, considered that the extent of the delay precluded granting relief for unfair prejudice.

In *Bailey v Cherry Hill Skip Hire Ltd* [2022] EWCA Civ 531; [2022] 2 B.C.L.C. 300, the Court of Appeal endorsed the approach to delay followed by Fancourt J in *Re Edwardian Group Ltd* [2018] EWHC 1715 (Ch); [2019] 1 B.C.L.C. 171 at [571]. The petitioner had been excluded from management and had through solicitors threatened to seek a winding-up order over 17 years before a petition was finally presented. The petition complained of a course of conduct over nearly four decades of exclusion from management and denial of his rights as a shareholder (particularly, as to company accounts, general meetings and dividends). The first instance judge dismissed the petition on the basis of delay, as a preliminary issue. The Court of Appeal reversed that. Although the petitioner could not realistically rely on his exclusion from management, there were allegations which were sufficiently recent so as not necessarily to be precluded by delay, particularly the petitioner's discovery, long after his exclusion, that money and/or corporate opportunities had been diverted from the company and his shareholding seemingly expropriated.

Replace the penultimate paragraph with:

If the petitioner is complicit in the conduct of which he complains, the court may deny them any relief in respect of that conduct. See *Hawkes v Cuddy* [2008] B.C.C. 390, where the petitioner was held to be hypocritical in complaining about the illegality of the company's affairs in which he was fully complicit.[133]

[133] A fortiori where the conduct complained of had been approved at the time by all the shareholders, including the trustees of the shares now held by the beneficiaries, that conduct could not later be relied upon as unfair prejudice: *Re Batesons Hotels (1958)* [2014] 1 B.C.L.C. 507. See also para.5-13. This passage was cited with approval in *Routledge v Skerritt* [2019] B.C.C. 812, a case concerned with the failure of the board to declare dividends: see para.7-71. On the facts, it was held that the petitioner had acquiesced in the wrongful conduct until he wrote to complain.

COLLATERAL PURPOSE OF PETITIONER

After the seventh paragraph, add a new paragraph:

In *Re Compound Photonics Group Ltd* [2020] EWHC 3176 (Ch); [2021] B.C.C. **7-88**
249, the petitioners alleged that the respondents had wrongfully excluded them from the management of the business in breach of the shareholders' agreement and articles. The respondents defended the petition on the basis that the petitioners had been negligent in the management of the business in breach of the same agreement, and counterclaimed for very substantial damages which were manifestly beyond the means of the petitioners. Shortly before trial, the respondents abandoned the counterclaim. The petitioners' application to debar the respondents from defending the petition failed, it being held that the respondents' conduct in maintaining an intimidatory counterclaim until the last minute did not amount to an abuse of process.

APPEALS

To the end of the last paragraph, add:

Cf. *Chu v Lau* [2020] UKPC 24; [2020] 1 W.L.R. 4656 at [70]; *Ming Siu Hung* **7-89**
v JF Ming Inc [2021] UKPC 1; [2021] B.C.C. 498 at [20]–[23], [32].

CHAPTER 8

Unfair Prejudice 2: Remedies

TABLE OF CONTENTS

FINAL ORDER

Jurisdiction

To the end of the first paragraph, add:

In *Re Gallium Funds Solutions Group Ltd* [2021] EWHC 765 (Ch), a trial as to valuation only had been ordered but subsequently a dispute arose as to whether the respondent had accepted that unfair prejudice was established and that the petitioner was entitled to a share purchase order. It was held, reference having been made to the need for a petitioner to establish unfair prejudice even in the absence of a defence or in the face of non-admissions as per *Bankside Hotels Ltd* [2018] EWHC 1035 (Ch), that the respondent had agreed that the petition would proceed to valuation without opposition and unfair prejudice was established by the matters referred to in the petition. The court nevertheless proceeded to make findings of fact, and findings of unfair prejudice based on those findings, as it would have done had the trial been of liability as well. **8-01**

THE COURT'S POWERS AND DISCRETION

Powers

To the end of the fifth paragraph, after "Bhullar v Bhullar unreported 10 May 2002", add:

Cf. *Fexuto Pty Ltd v Bosjnak Holdings Pty Ltd* (2001) 37 ACSR 672 at [212]–[213]; *Hawkes v Cuddy (No.2)* [2007] EWHC 2999 (Ch); [2008] B.C.C. 390 at **8-05**

[250] and *Liu Tieh Ching Brandon v Liu Ju Ching* [2021] HKCFI 823; [2021] HKEC 1227 at [39]–[42].

Discretion

Purpose of remedy

To the end of the last paragraph, add:

8-06 In *Re Macom GmBH (UK) Ltd* [2021] EWHC 1661 (Ch), the Court considered that the Court's discretion as to remedy was not limited to that which was sought in the petition (nor any cross-petition), irrespective of whether the prayer to the petition included general words such as 'such other order as the Court thinks fit.', that conclusion being supported by the reasoning in *Hawkes v Cuddy*. Thus, the court can order relief other than that which the petitioner seeks, although the petitioner's opposition to any other relief is something for the court to take into consideration.

A clean break

After the last paragraph, add a new paragraph:

8-08 In *Ming Siu Hung v JF Ming Inc* [2021] UKPC 1; [2021] B.C.C. 498 at [17], the Privy Council considered that there was no useful purpose in attempting to describe the types of case in which a buy-out order is the usual remedy, in circumstances where the legislation, rather than indicating a preferred remedy in any particular case, confers a wide discretion.

The material time

Replace the paragraph with:

8-10 The relevant time for determining whether an order should be made under s.994 is the date of hearing of the petition, not the date of its presentation: *Grace v Biagioli* [2006] B.C.C. 85 at [73].[19] Accordingly, conduct after the presentation of the petition and before the hearing may in principle, subject to the usual rules as to amendments to pleadings, be relied upon in support of the petition. Events taking place after the presentation of the petition are in any event relevant and admissible on the issue of the appropriate remedy. In *Cheung Hon Wah v Cheung Kam Wah* [2005] HKEC 765 it was held that in Hong Kong, by analogy with other ordinary actions (the *Eshelby* rule), amendments should not generally be allowed in respect of new matters which had arisen since the presentation of the petition and did not arise out of already pleaded causes of action. The better course was for the petitioner to issue a fresh petition. Any such rule is likely to be confined to Hong Kong. In *Chu v Lau* [2020] UKPC 24; [2020] 1 W.L.R. 4656 at [41]–[43], a BVI appeal, it was observed that the *Eshelby* rule had been discarded in the UK, and further held that it had no application in any event to proceedings for a just and equitable winding-up and also by implication unfair prejudice petitions, and therefore amendments to add new allegations of unfair prejudice based on events after the presentation of the petition may be allowed on the usual conditions. In *Re Hailey Group Ltd*,[20] the petitioner had originally sought an order that the respondents sell their shares to him but, following the appointment of administrative receivers, sought instead an order that the respondents purchase his shares. It was held that he was not entitled to such an order, since it would be tantamount to imposing a fine on the respondents. The learned judge envisaged circumstances where supervening insolvency would not prevent the making of such an order, for example where the unfairly prejudicial conduct had prevented the petitioner from selling his shares at a proper price prior to the onset of insolvency. If a petitioner is entitled to an order that his shares be purchased and the appropriate date of valuation is before the onset of insolvency, the onset of insolvency should be irrelevant, save possibly as relevant to the issue of valuation.

[19] The same principle applies to winding up on the just and equitable basis: *Jenkins v Supascaf* [2006] 3 N.Z.L.R. 264.

[20] *Re Hailey Group Ltd* [1992] B.C.C. 542 Ch D. See also *Re Fildes Bros* [1970] 1 All E.R. 923 Ch D at 927d.

After the first paragraph, add new paragraphs:

In *Ming Siu Hung v JF Ming Inc* [2021] UKPC 1; [2021] B.C.C. 498 at [14], the following principles were endorsed as being essentially common ground between counsel:

> "First, the court is entitled to have regard to any aspect of the facts as found about the history of the company and the relationship between its shareholders inter se, and between them and the directors, including those occurring after the issue of the claim and those which may fairly be found by the court even though not necessarily pleaded. In short, nothing is off-limits, subject only to the twin tests of relevance and weight, in relation to the choices to be made in the exercise of the discretion. Secondly, the court necessarily looks not only to the past but to what the court finds is likely to happen in the future."

Cf. *Financial Technology Ventures II (Q) LP v ETFS Capital Ltd* [2021] JCA 176 at [47].

In *Re Motion Pictures Capital Ltd* [2021] EWHC 2504 (Ch); [2022] B.C.C. 62, it was said at [47]:

> "The trial judge has a wide discretion under CA section 996 regarding the remedy, but must fashion it according to the unfair prejudice found. He or she may also take into account, if relevant, conduct that has taken place after the date of presentation of the petition as well as conduct occurring prior to that date. Further, a judge at trial is not restricted to granting the remedy claimed by a petitioner, if he or she considers that that remedy is not appropriate to the findings of unfair prejudice made."

Cf. *Chu v Lau* [2020] UKPC 24; [2020] 1 W.L.R. 4656 at [43] as to just and equitable winding-up: "the court should consider all relevant matters as at the date of the hearing."

ORDERS IN FAVOUR OF THE MAJORITY

After the last paragraph, add new paragraphs:

In *Albion Energy Ltd v Energy Investments Global BRL* [2020] EWHC 301 (Comm); [2020] 1 Lloyd's Rep. 501, a claim by the majority shareholders that they were entitled to relief under ss.994–996 as respects payments alleged to have been wrongfully made in breach of director's duty was held to be hopeless, since the majority shareholders could cause the company to pursue such a claim itself. **8-12**

Re Integrated Control Solutions (Eastern) Ltd [2021] EWHC 1374 (Ch) concerned a company in which two individuals (Mr M and Mr H) and their spouses each held 25% shareholdings. Mr H had secretly operated a competing business, which Mr M discovered. Mr H contended, however, that Mr M, together with Mrs M and Mrs H, from whom he had separated, unfairly excluded him from management. When Mr M presented his petition (which sought an order that Mr H sell his 25% shareholding to him valued subject to a minority discount), Mr M and Mr H were the two directors, but Mr H later resigned. The Court rejected an argument that Mr M could not rely in his petition on Mr H's misconduct on the footing that Mr M was in sole control of the business and "de facto majority shareholder", although this may be relevant to the question of relief, distinguishing authorities such as *Re Legal Costs Negotiators Ltd* [1999] B.C.C. 547; [1999] 2 B.C.L.C. 171 on the basis that those did not deal with a situation where the position had changed since the petition was presented. The position was, however, different as respects amendments introduced during the currency of the petition, which were treated as not capable of properly being treated as unfairly prejudicial, since they were allegations which the petitioner should have caused the company to pursue.

A petition by the majority (60%) shareholder in *Re Macom GMBH (UK) Ltd* [2021] EWHC 1661(Ch) was allowed to proceed in circumstances where, by the terms of a shareholders' agreement, one of the minority shareholders had a casting vote as respects a board of two directors.

THE PERSONS AGAINST WHOM RELIEF MAY BE GRANTED

Replace the first paragraph with:

8-13 The normal persons against whom relief may be granted are the current members of the company, particularly those who bear the requisite degree of responsibility for the unfair prejudice suffered by the petitioner: see *Re Baltic Real Estate (No.1)* [1993] B.C.L.C. 498. There may be circumstances, however, where an order may be made against past members: *Re Company (No.005287 of 1985)* [1986] B.C.L.C. 68 Ch D (Companies Ct) at 71e–f. There are also cases where orders may be made against or directly affecting persons who have never been members: *Re BSB Holdings Ltd* [1992] B.C.C. 915 Ch D (Companies Ct). Further, the court has power under ss.994–996 to make any order that it could have made if the proceedings had instead been brought as a derivative action, including an order for the payment in favour of the company by way of compensation for any loss suffered or by way of an account of profits, and in particular orders against third parties who have been properly joined as parties for this purpose: see paras 8-20–8-24 and 9-17. Thus, for example, in *Re The Hut Group Ltd* [2021] EWCA Civ 904; [2021] B.C.C. 970 at [66], it was held that the powers under s.996 plainly include the power to order wrongdoing directors to pay compensation to the petitioner. A derivative claim against a non-director under the new statutory code must arise out of a director's breach; if it does not, it can only be brought with the court's sanction under s.996(2)(c)[22]: *Iesini v Westrip Holdings Ltd* [2010] B.C.C. 420 per Lewison J; see para.6-09.

[22] In *SDI Retail Services Ltd v King* [2017] EWHC 737 (Ch) at [49], it was held that the derivative claim against a third party did not arise independently of the directors' breach of duty and therefore could be brought under the statutory regime.

SPECIFIC REMEDIES

Share purchase orders

General

To the end of the first paragraph, add:

8-16 In *Ming Siu Hung v JF Ming Inc* [2021] UKPC 1; [2021] B.C.C. 498 at [17], the board observed that the legislation did not make a buy-out a preferred remedy either generally or in particular circumstances and declined to indicate particular circumstances where a buy-out order might be the usual remedy. Cf. *Financial Technology Ventures II (Q) LP v ETFS Capital Ltd* [2021] JCA 176 at [62].

After the last paragraph, add new paragraphs:

In *Re Stratos Club* [2020] EWHC 3485 (Ch) at [359]–[362], a share purchase order was made by reference to a percentage share of a notional top company in order to capture that the companies in which the petitioner held shares was essentially a single business and the sum of the parts likely had a value which was greater than the whole.

In *Russell v Lee Holdings Pty Ltd (No.3)* [2020] WASC 346, in the context of unusual facts and admitted oppression, the Court directed, with the concurrence of the parties, a mutual offer process, the essential characteristic (somewhat simplified to pass over complexities arising from an unusual corporate structure) of which was that each of two factions (one faction comprising the elderly mother, who held a single 'super-share' conferring supreme overall control of the whole structure, together with one child owning one-third of the other shares; and the other faction, comprising the two other children holding approximately two-thirds of the other shares) could submit to the Court a price per share bid and the highest bidder, if any, would acquire the other side's shares at a price corresponding to their bid. If there was no highest bidder, there would be a winding-up order on the just-and-equitable ground.

Interim payment on account of share purchase

After the last paragraph, add a new paragraph:

In *Re Stratos Club* [2021] EWHC 1008 (Ch), the Court confirmed that there is power under CPR r.25.1(1)(k) and CPR r.25.7(1)(b) and also under s.996 of the Companies Act 2006 to make an order for payment on account of a price to be paid where a share purchase order has been made after the liability trial but before the valuation. The Court made an order for an interim payment of an amount which it was satisfied was very unlikely to be more than that which would be allowed at the valuation trial. **8-17**

Order that respondents sell to petitioner

After the last paragraph, add a new paragraph:

In *Cheyne v Alfred Cheyne Engineering Ltd* [2021] CSOH 17, the Outer House rejected a submission that the default remedy is for the majority to purchase the minority's shares. This is an appropriate remedy in many but not all circumstances. For this reason (among others), an application to strike out the petition, which relied on an offer by the majority including an offer to purchase the minorities' shares (at market value on a non-discounted basis), failed. A key consideration was that the petitioners, the minority, held an option which was yet to mature to acquire the majority's shares. **8-18**

Interest on the price payable under a share purchase order

After the last paragraph, add a new paragraph:

In *Re Sprintroom Ltd* [2020] EWHC 3465 (Ch) at [51]–[60], quasi-interest at 3% was ordered on an adjusting payment to the share purchase price (referred to in the judgment as the 'balancing payment' to reflect that after the petitioner's exclusion, he (through his company) had not received his 40% share of payments for **8-19** services provided by the company—see [5] and [56]). The question of quasi-interest on the share purchase price itself was postponed: see [141].

The remedying of wrongs to the company—breach of duty by directors

Order in favour of the petitioner

After the last paragraph, add new paragraphs:

8-22 In *Re The Hut Group Ltd* [2021] EWCA Civ 904; [2021] B.C.C. 970 at [66], it was held that s.996 plainly included a power to order wrongdoing directors to pay compensation to a petitioner, such a power not being dependent upon a fiduciary or statutory duty being owed by the directors to the petitioner personally.

In *Re Weir Travel Ltd* [2021] NICh 18, the Court considered it clear that an order under s.996 could be made for the payment of compensation by the respondents to the petitioner and/or to the company, and made orders as respects both: an order for payment to the petitioner by the respondents of that amount of what they had received as dividends which should have been paid to the petitioner; and repayment by the respondents to the company of excessive remuneration.

Orders for future regulation of company's affairs

After the last paragraph, add new paragraphs:

8-23 In *Re Macom GmBH (UK) Ltd* [2021] EWHC 1661 (Ch), an order to regulate the companies' affairs (requiring, e.g. strict adherence to the articles and shareholders' agreement, decisions to be taken by the board, regular board meetings and proper minutes) was considered to be the appropriate order where the unfair prejudice related to the governance of the company's affairs and had not been shown to have caused financial loss and it was unlikely that the respondent had the means to satisfy a share purchase order.

See too *Cheyne v Alfred Cheyne Engineering Ltd* [2021] CSOH 17, where an application to strike out the petition, which relied on an offer by the majority which included an offer to purchase the minorities' shares (at market value and on a non-discounted basis), failed. It was not inevitable that a share purchase order would be made rather than a form of regulation of the affairs of the company. In that case, the petitioners held an option which was soon to mature to acquire the majority's shares, which might, following trial, tend to favour regulation of the affairs as an appropriate remedy over a share purchase order (and the petition sought, among other relief, an order for the purchase by the petitioners of the majority's shares and not a sale of the petitioners' shares).

Petitions founded on personal causes of action

Replace the last paragraph with:

8-24 In *Re Hut Group Ltd* [2020] EWHC 5 (Ch), the court declined to strike out a petition based on breaches of duty by the directors and also the relief claimed by way of an order for payment of equitable compensation to the company and the petitioner personally. On appeal, [2020] EWHC 5 (Ch); [2021] B.C.C. 970, parts of the petition were struck out, including part of the prayer claiming an order that the directors pay equitable compensation to the company, but the basis for that seems to have been that the complaints (or those which survived) were not ones where it could be said that the directors had caused loss to the company. Compensation for such losses could be ordered directly by the wrongdoing directors to the petitioners under s.996.

OFFERS TO BUY OUT AT INDEPENDENT VALUATION

An "O'Neill v Phillips offer"

Replace the second paragraph with:

In *Re Sprintroom Ltd* [2018] EWHC 1924 (Ch) at [386]; appeal dismissed [2019] EWCA Civ 932, the issue arose whether the court, having at the trial on liability held that the petitioner was entitled to a share purchase order, should nevertheless decline to grant that relief, at least until the valuation had taken place, as a result of what were alleged to be reasonable offers made for his shares by the respondents over the period of the dispute. The Court of Appeal held that none of the offers should have stood in the way of the court making a share purchase order: **8-29**

- the first offers were made at a time when the relationship had not yet broken down irretrievably: at [136], [141];
- the next offer provided that no account be taken of one of the petitioner's allegations of misappropriation of assets, which had yet to be determined: at [133], [142];
- an offer of a fixed price was only open for 21 days: at [131]–[132], [143]–[144]; and
- it was relevant to consider any doubts as to the ability of the offeror to fund the purchase: at [134]–[135].[48]

[48] A petitioner is not obliged to accept an offer which is expressed to be conditional on the affordability of the price ultimately determined by the expert: *Re Flex Associates Ltd* [2009] EWHC 3690 (Ch).

After the second paragraph, add new paragraphs:

In *Cheyne v Alfred Cheyne Engineering Ltd* [2021] CSOH 17 at [59]–[65], the court declined to strike out a petition following an offer to purchase (or sell) as (i) there was a real possibility that the appropriate relief would be a reverse buy-out; and (ii) the offer to sell was not necessarily a fair price. A key consideration was that the petitioners (30% shareholders) held an option which had not yet matured to acquire the respondents' shares (70% shareholders).

See *Birchfield v Birchfield Holdings Ltd* [2021] NZCA 3020 and *Hiscock v Panmure Orchards Ltd* [2021] NZHC 3020 following *Re Sprintroom Ltd* [2019] EWCA Civ 932; [2019] B.C.C. 1031. In *Birchfield v Birchfield Holdings Ltd* [2021] NZCA 3020 at [39], the following factors were said to be relevant to the Court's assessment of the reasonableness of an offer:

(a) the value offered, or the means proposed for arriving at that value;
(b) the ability of the claimant to satisfy themselves that the figure offered is reasonable before they have to decide whether to accept or reject the offer;
(c) the substance of the unfair prejudice allegations, and the implications of those allegations for the assessment of fair value;
(d) the likelihood of the majority shareholder being able to implement the offer made;
(e) the proximity of the offer to the unfairly prejudicial conduct complained of.

It was said at [40] that the question of whether an offer renders an unfair prejudice claim bound to fail was highly sensitive to the facts and circumstances and that the Court should be cautious of summary disposal. On an application for summary disposal the relevant offer(s) should be those which had been made when the application was made; it would usually be unfair to the respondent to such an application to require them to deal with a moving feast, particularly if that affected the evidential playing field. But there was no absolute bar to summary disposal on the basis of an offer(s) which evolved during the course of the application. In the result, in *Birchfield* an adjusted offer would be sufficient to fully address any arguable claims of unfair prejudice; an opportunity was given to make that offer; and the dismissal of the claim would be upheld. In *Hiscock v Panmure Orchards Ltd* [2021] NZHC 3020, an application for summary disposal was refused, on the basis that the claimant had a claim as respects remuneration which could affect valuation and should be determined by the Court (rather than being suitable for expert determination, even with the assistance of legal advice). But the Court encouraged the parties to try to deal with the remuneration issue separately, with the remaining issues capable of being addressed by a valuer.

In *Loveridge v Loveridge* [2021] EWCA Civ 1697; [2022] B.C.C. 324, which concerned a caravan park business carried on by five 'family' companies, the allegations of unfair prejudice were found to be unarguable as respects all but one company and as respects that company there was an *O'Neill v Phillips* offer which provided all the relief to which the petitioner could be entitled as respects that company. Thus, the petition was struck out in its entirety.

Where split trials of liability and quantum are ordered, and a Pt 36 or other relevant offer or payment has been made to a petitioner who has succeeded on liability, the normal order is "costs reserved": *Dinglis v Dinglis* [2019] Costs L.R. 1909.

After the last paragraph, add a new paragraph:

In *Somerville v McGuire* [2020] CSOH 70 at [50]–[53], the Outer House considered (obiter) the extent of the right to information conferred by Lord Hoffmann's fourth "equality of arms" principle in *O'Neill v Phillips*: while the words "information about the company which bears upon the value of the shares" indicates that a party does not have a full and unfettered right of information to any information whatsoever which he wishes to see, nevertheless the parties should be entitled to the same right of access. Thus, in the instant case, it was seen to be important that the expert could access information which either party believed to be relevant to valuation, without any threshold of a need to be persuaded by the parties that it was in fact relevant to valuation.

Delegation to valuer of issues of principle

Replace the penultimate paragraph with:

8-30 There have been, however, cases where the courts have held the offer to be reasonable even though it delegated to the valuer the right to determine issues relevant to valuation which involved issues of fact or law or both, including what allowance should be made for unfairly prejudicial conduct: *Re Company (No.00836 of 1995)* [1996] B.C.C. 432; *Re Company (No.003843 of 1986)* (1987) 3 B.C.C. 624. If a respondent wishes to strike out a petition on the basis that a fair offer has been made for the petitioner's shares, he is accepting an obligation to buy out the petitioner's shares at the value determined by the independent expert on a specified basis. The court, in the exercise of its discretion, may in an appropriate case allow to be delegated to the valuer any subsidiary issue of law, or issue of mixed law and fact, which is relevant to the valuation. So, it may be desirable to draft an offer so as to give the valuer the express right to take legal advice on legal issues, or from an expert on other issues. If, therefore, a common obstacle to an offer of an out-of-court valuation is that there may be particular issues arising in the case which are not appropriate for determination save by the court or in the context of a court valuation, in such a case the court would have power to reserve such issues for preliminary determination, whilst leaving the valuation to be carried out by an independent expert: see, e.g. *Re Clearsprings (Management)* [2003] EWHC 2516 (Ch).

After the penultimate paragraph, add a new paragraph:

The text of the above paragraph from "The court, in the exercise of its discretion..." to the end of it was cited with approval in *Hiscock v Panmure Orchards Ltd* [2021] NZHC 3020 at [41]: the relevant issue (a claim as respects remuneration) was not considered suitable for expert determination and, therefore, summary disposal on the basis of an *O'Neill v Phillips* offer was refused, but the Court encouraged the parties to arrange for this claim to be dealt with as discrete issue, to pave the way for expert determination of the remaining valuation issues.

INTERIM INJUNCTIVE RELIEF

Jurisdiction

To the end of the first paragraph, add:

See now *Broad Idea International Ltd v Convoy Collateral Ltd* [2021] UKPC 24; **8-39**
[2022] 2 W.L.R. 703, affirming the *Chabra* jurisdiction and stating that the purpose of a freezing injunction is to facilitate the enforcement of a judgment or other order to pay a sum of money and there is no reason to link the grant of such an injunction to the existence of a cause of action.

Discretion: American Cyanamid adapted to the relief sought

Examples

After the last paragraph, add new paragraphs:

In *Re Premiere Care Holdings Ltd* [2021] EWHC 1595 (Ch), the Court refused **8-41**
to grant an interim injunction to remove current directors from the board, such that the petitioner should have sole control of the company, referring to *Re A Company* [1985] B.C.L.C. 80, and emphasising that it was not clear that the petitioner would obtain control of the company as a result of the final relief which he sought. The Court nevertheless required certain undertakings to regulate the affairs of the company pending trial, including regular minuted board meetings, limits on the incurring of liabilities and no declarations of dividends.

In *MI Squared Ltd v King* [2022] EWHC 331 (Comm); [2022] 2 B.C.L.C. 279, the Court refused an injunction to prevent directors, without the approval of the majority shareholder, from paying off any indebtedness of the company or its subsidiaries, incurring any new indebtedness or encumbering any assets of the company or its subsidiaries, given that there was no sufficiently strong case that a new loan would breach a shareholders' agreement or that the directors would be in breach of their duties in entering into it. Given that the application was likely to be determinative of a battle between the majority shareholders, who were also substantial creditors and favoured an administration, and the board who had found funding which would stave off the administration, the Court went further than merely considering whether there was a serious question to be tried and considered the relative merits of the arguments by reference to the guidance in *Forse v Secarma Ltd* [2019] EWCA Civ 215 at [34].

Appointment of provisional liquidators

After the last paragraph, add new paragraph:

In *Re Debenhams Plc* [2020] EWHC 1755 (Ch), the Court declined to appoint **8-42**
provisional liquidators on a "without notice" application in a contributory's petition, where the purpose of the appointment for the provisional liquidators was to

investigate a pre-pack sale (with the provisional liquidators to be funded by the petitioners). The Court considered that the appointment of provisional liquidators remained a "draconian" order, even where the company was not trading and had no assets. The Court was concerned that the effect of such an order would be to impose the petitioners' choice of office holders on the company. The application was adjourned, to be heard together with the hearing of the petition.

Freezing orders

The assets of individual respondents

Replace paragraph with:

8-43 If the petitioner seeks Mareva-type freezing orders against individual respondents and their assets, he must establish a cause of action against them in order to provide the basis for such an injunction against them: *Re Premier Electronics (GB) Ltd* [2002] 2 B.C.L.C. 634 Ch D.[68] *Sed quaere*. Yet a third party, against whom no substantive claim in the petition exists, can be joined as a respondent for the purpose of granting an injunction against it which is ancillary and incidental to a claim in the petition against another respondent: *TSB Private Bank International v Chabra* [1992] 1 W.L.R. 231. See now *Broad Idea International Ltd v Convoy Collateral Ltd* [2021] UKPC 24; [2022] 2 W.L.R. 703, affirming the *Chabra* jurisdiction and stating that the purpose of a freezing injunction is to facilitate the enforcement of a judgment or other order to pay a sum of money and there is no reason to link the grant of such an injunction to the existence of a cause of action.

[68] It may well be that this decision turned on the particular facts of the case since the company had been put into administration on the petition of persons associated with the petitioners. So, it may well be that the petitioners, as shareholders, lacked any standing to bring proceedings for relief against the individual respondents for the return of the misappropriated assets: only the administrators could do so: see the observations of Lord Scott in *Re Chime Corp Ltd* [2004] 7 HKCFAR 546 at para.7-60.

After the first paragraph, add a new paragraph:

In *Kumar v Sharma* [2022] EWHC 612 (Ch) at [45]–[48], it was held that while a share buyout order was not a money judgment, it is still an order requiring a person to pay money. Therefore, there should be jurisdiction to make a freezing order. The Court referred to *Palmer v Lovelight* Unreported, 16 August 2017, in which Warren J had continued a freezing injunction in respect of an individual against whom a share buyout order was sought in unfair prejudice proceedings. *Re Cloud Employee Ltd (No.09039315)* [2020] EWHC 848 (Ch) is another example. Although not referred to, the broader jurisprudential basis for freezing relief elucidated in *Broad Idea International Ltd v Convoy Collateral Ltd* [2021] UKPC 24; [2022] 2 W.L.R. 703 supports the view that there is no bar to seeking freezing order relief in the context of an unfair prejudice petition claiming a buyout order.

VALUATION OF SHARES

General

Replace the first paragraph with:

8-45 This is a very wide and specialist subject, on which one would be tempted to defer to the expertise of share valuers. This temptation is to be resisted, however, because there are questions of law and principle involved in the present context, share valuation is an art not a science (*Joiner v George* [2003] B.C.C. 298), and a court retains a wide freedom to disregard the views of experts and apply the court's view of what is fair and sensible in all the circumstances: *Re Bird Precision Bellows* [1986] Ch. 658 at 669; *Re Planet Organic Ltd* [2000] B.C.C. 610 Ch D. Cf. *Re Solent Garages Ltd* [2020] EWHC 1975 (Ch) at [19]; *Otello Corp ASA v Moore Frères and Co LLC* [2020] EWHC 3261 (Ch); *Re Sprintroom Ltd* [2020] EWHC 3465 (Ch) at [15]; *Re Icamera Ltd* [2021] EWHC 1762 (Ch) at [32]. In *Financial Technology Ventures II (Q) LP v ETFS Capital Ltd* [2021] JCA 176 at [62], the Jersey Court of Appeal held:

> "... In fixing the price at which a plaintiff's shares are to be acquired, the court is not conducting a 'valuation' as such. In other words, it is not performing an objective, mathematical exercise dictated by the expert evidence and by reference to accountancy principles alone. Instead, it is conducting an evaluation. In other words, it is performing a remedial function involving a judgment call which is made in light of all the circumstances of the case and by reference to principles of fairness ..."

and cf. [169]–[170].

After the first paragraph, add a new paragraph:

The courts have occasionally deprecated the emergence of a new breed of professional expert valuers whose principal experience lies in acting as an expert witness. The view of an expert valuer will generally carry greater weight with the court if it is supported by objective evidence in the form of personal practical experience in buying and selling business of the type in question, in other words the experience to be found in the corporate finance department.[70] Valuation methodologies based more on theory than verifiable evidence may, depending upon the circumstances and the availability of other methodologies, carry less weight with the court: see, e.g. *Taylor v Cobham & Lifemarque Ltd* [2009] EWHC 2650 (Ch).

[70] See *Re Sunrise Radio Ltd* [2011] EWHC 3821 (Ch) at [5].

In the first sentence of the last paragraph, after "share purchase order," add:

and often the greatest impediment to settlement,

Earnings v assets

To the end of the third paragraph, after "apparently well-run business.", add:

See too *Otello Corp ASA v Moore Frères and Co LLC* [2020] EWHC 3261 (Ch) at [216]–[219] where the Court expressed some preference for an earnings and multiplier based methodology rather than discounted cash-flows, but considered both to be unreliable, preferring instead to base valuation on the price actually offered at arm's length by a third-party. **8-47**

ISSUES ARISING IN VALUATION

(i) Discount for a minority shareholding

Quasi-partnership

Replace footnote 93 with:

[93] See *Re Bird Precision Bellows* [1984] Ch. 419 at 430D-F; [1986] Ch. 658 at 673H–674B. See also *Re Company (No.000789 of 1987)* [1990] B.C.L.C. 384 and [1991] B.C.L.C. 267; *Virdi v Abbey Leisure* [1990] B.C.L.C. 342; *Ex p. Holden* [1991] B.C.C. 241; *Howie v Crawford* [1990] B.C.L.C. 686 Ch D at 690e–691e; *Re Ghyll Beck Driving Range* [1993] B.C.L.C. 1126; and *Quinlan v Essex Hinge Co Ltd* [1997] B.C.C. 53 Ch D (Companies Ct); *Strahan v Wilcox* [2006] B.C.C. 320 at [17]; *Re Sprintroom Ltd* [2018] EWHC 1924 (Ch); appeal dismissed [2019] EWCA Civ 932 at [89]–[95]. In the unusual circumstances of *Re Integrated Control Solutions (Eastern) Ltd* [2021] EWHC 1374 (Ch), where the **8-53**

petitioner, a 25% shareholder, obtained an order for the purchase of a quasi-partner's shares (not the sale of his own), also a 25% shareholding, a minority discount was applied: it was the respondent quasi-partner whose conduct (secretly carrying on a competing business) had destroyed the quasi-partnership.

Other relationships—the norm

After the last paragraph, add new paragraphs:

8-55 At a subsequent hearing in the same proceedings, *Dinglis v Dinglis* [2019] EWHC 3327 (Ch); [2020] 2 B.C.L.C. 574, the Court, having regard to what was said in *Re Edwardian Group Ltd* [2018] EWHC 1715 (Ch) that assessing a fair value did not necessarily entail choosing between the extremes of no minority discount and a "fully discounted" valuation, was prepared to consider various matters as potentially impacting on the size of the discount. In the result, the only matter which was considered as properly capable of doing so was the potential marriage value to the purchasing shareholder, such that the shares should be valued on the basis of a notional sale between the actual parties in question, and not on the basis of a sale to an independent third party.

In *Otello Corp ASA v Moore Frères and Co LLC* [2020] EWHC 3261 (Ch) at [237]–[255], following a review of the authorities, the Court expressed doubt whether the Court should approach the question from the point of view of any rule or principle that a minority discount should or should not apply in a case which was not a quasi-partnership. Rather the question was what was fair and equitable in the circumstances, which, in a case which was not a quasi-partnership, may or may not be a non-discounted valuation.

Similarly, in *Financial Technology Ventures II (Q) LP v ETFS Capital Ltd* [2021] JCA 176 at [173]–[177], taking into account English authority (and that of other jurisdictions) but in circumstances where such authority was not binding on the Jersey Court of Appeal, it was held that there were no inflexible rules as to whether a minority discount should be awarded in any given case, with context such as whether a company was a quasi-partnership and whether the petitioner was only seeking to be bought out reluctantly are factors to be capable of being taken into account. The court declined to interfere with the judge's assessment that prima facie a discount of 40% should be applied but that, given the purchaser was an existing shareholder, this should be reduced to 20% to reflect the marriage value.

Replace the first paragraph with:

8-56 The view that, if the company is not a quasi-partnership, there must be exceptional circumstances before a shareholding is valued without a discount appears to be based on analogies with other contexts where the courts have to value minority shareholdings. First, in the law of partnership, where a partnership falls to be dissolved on the just and equitable basis, each partner is entitled to a pro rata share of the value of net assets including goodwill, ascertained by a valuation or an order for sale: *Syers v Syers* (1876) 1 App. Cas. 174 (see para.8-27 on the partnership analogy). Secondly, there are a number of statutory provisions, in the UK and the Cayman Islands,[100] which enable a majority shareholder in certain circumstances, subject to some degree of control by the court, to squeeze out, i.e. force to sell, minority shareholders. In contrast to other jurisdictions in North America with similar "squeeze out" provisions, under English and Cayman Islands law, minority shareholdings are valued with a discount for their minority status: *Shanda Games Ltd v Maso Capital Investments Ltd* [2020] UKPC 2; [2020] B.C.C. 466, discussed in detail in Ch.13. Cf. *Re Euro Accessories Ltd* [2021] EWHC 47 (Ch) applying the reasoning in *Shanda* to a right of compulsory expropriation conferred by the company's articles.

[100] Discussed in Ch.13.

After the last paragraph, add a new paragraph:

In *Senda International Capital Ltd v Kiri Industries Ltd* [2020] WGCA(I) 01 it was held that there is no presumption that a discount applies where the company is not a quasi-partnership, following *Thio Syn Pyn v Thio Syn Kym Wendy* [2019] 1 S.L.R. 1065. The Singapore Court of Appeal upheld an order for the purchase of the minority's shares on a non-discounted basis, where the company was not a quasi-partnership and the majority shareholder's oppressive conduct had been responsible for the breakdown in the parties' relationship.

(iv) Date of valuation

General

After the quote, add a new paragraph:

In *Financial Technology Ventures II (Q) LP v ETFS Capital Ltd* [2021] JCA 176, **8-60** the Jersey Court of Appeal, while noting the observations in *Profinance Trust v Gladstone* [2001] EWCA Civ 1031; [2002] 1 W.L.R. 1024 to the effect that the starting point should be a valuation as at the date of the purchase order for a going concern business, held that given that the ultimate question was that of fairness, there were no fixed rules as to valuation date for the purposes of the similar unfair prejudice remedy in Jersey.

Examples

Replace list with:

- *Re Adlink* unreported 17 October 2006—the date of Heads of Agreement prior to the commencement of proceedings; **8-61**
- *Taylor v Cobham & Lifemarque Ltd* [2009] EWHC 2650 (Ch)—the date of the court order;
- *Croly v Good* [2011] B.C.C. 105—the date of expulsion which caused him unfair prejudice, because the respondent had failed to disclose all necessary financial information which would have been needed to dispel the suspicion that the fortunes of the company had been manipulated so as to diminish its value following the expulsion: at [113]. This reasoning was applied in *Shepherd v Phoenix Contracts (Leicester) Ltd* [2010] EWHC 2375 (Ch);
- *Re KR Hardy Estates Ltd* [2016] B.C.C. 367—the date of the court order;
- *Pinfold v Ansell* [2017] 2 B.C.L.C. 489—the date of exclusion of the quasi-partner, because since then he had been locked into a business which was pursuing a commercial strategy from which he was excluded; and
- *Re CF Booth Ltd* [2017] EWHC 457 (Ch)—a date before the fall in value of a loss-making company.
- *Re Stratos Club* [2020] EWHC 3485 (Ch)—a date which reflected the time when the petitioner was in effect deprived of her share in the business, but postponed such that the valuation would take into account the benefit of the acquisition of a further club.
- *Re Icamera Ltd* [2021] EWHC 1762 (Ch)—a date immediately before the misappropriation of the business to a new vehicle.
- *Re Integrated Control Solutions (Eastern) Ltd* [2021] EWHC 1374 (Ch), where a quasi-partner had been found out to have secretly carried on business in competition with the company, a date some months after the date on which it was clear that the parties could no longer continue in business together, but long before the trial. A current valuation would not be fair as

the other principal quasi-partner had been treating the company as his own for that long period.

After the last paragraph, add new paragraphs:

In *Dinglis v Dinglis* [2019] EWHC 3327 (Ch); [2020] 2 B.C.L.C. 574, the Court rejected the suggestion that the valuation should be at an early date because a current valuation would allow the petitioner to reap the rewards of efforts said to have been primarily those of one of the respondents: the petitioner had been effectively locked in as a shareholder and was entitled to the benefit of the company's improved fortunes. The Court also rejected an argument that there should be an early valuation on the basis of delay: while delay could justify such a course, as had been held in *Re Edwardian Group Ltd* [2018] EWHC 1715 (Ch), the alleged delay must be measured as against the pursuit of the allegations of unfair prejudice which succeeded (and not those which have failed) and on the facts there was no culpable delay in that respect. A share purchase order was made on the basis of a current valuation (viz. the date on which the order was made, following the liability trial, but before the valuation trial).

At a subsequent hearing in the same case, *Dinglis v Dinglis* [2020] EWHC 1363 (Ch); [2020] 2 B.C.L.C. 607, it was suggested that the coronavirus pandemic had adversely affected the business and this was something which should be taken into account in assessing the share purchase price, either by revisiting the valuation date or by adjusting the price to similar effect. The Court, while accepting that the jurisdiction under s.996(1) is a very broad one which in principle is to be exercised at all points (even after trial) until the Court's order is carried into full effect, rejected the suggestion that the order be revisited so as to bring into account matters after the valuation date fixed therein.

Evidence

Replace the first paragraph with:

8-62 In fixing the material date of valuation, the court will take into account any changes over time in factors relevant to valuation (see paras 8-60–8-61), but, once once the date of valuation has been fixed, this will generally render immaterial and purposely so, for example, any change in the relevant market after the valuation date. As a matter of general valuation practice, but subject always to the overriding objective of arriving at a fair valuation in this context (see para.8-45), the courts will eschew so far as practicable wisdom with the benefit of hindsight.[108]

[108] The post-valuation date exclusionary rule in the context of valuations is to be contrasted with the case of quantification of damages for breach of warranty: per Blair J in *Hut Group Ltd v Nobahar-Cookson* [2014] EWHC 3842 (QB) at [181]. See also per Arden LJ (dissenting in the result) at [45] in the decision of the Court of Appeal in *Gorne v Scales* [2006] EWCA Civ 311, applying *Bwllfa and Merthy Dare Steam Collieries (1891) Ltd v Pontypridd Waterworks Co* [1903] A.C. 426 HL at 431: the general principle is that, where the court is charged with determining the value of an income-earning asset at a particular date and the valuation falls to be made at a time when it is known what income was in fact earned, the court should take into account the information as to the profits actually earned. The judgment in *Re Sprintroom Ltd* [2020] EWHC 3465 (Ch) at [11]–[28] contains a valuable summary of the rival submissions, with which the judge did not express any disagreement, as to the purpose of the valuation exercise, including the extent to which post valuation date events could and should be taken into account.

Valuations outside a petition

The role of the court

To the end of the second paragraph, add:

8-67 Cf. *Re Euro Accessories Ltd* [2021] EWHC 47 (Ch), in which it was held, by analogy with *Shanda Games Ltd v Maso Capital Investments Ltd* [2020] UKPC 2;

[2020] B.C.C. 466, that a right to purchase a minority shareholding conferred by a company's articles for '*fair value*' did not connote a pro rata valuation, rather than a valuation with a discount for a minority shareholding.

CHAPTER 9

Unfair Prejudice 3: Practice and Procedure

TABLE OF CONTENTS

LOCUS STANDI

Member

After the last paragraph, add a new paragraph:

See *Kumar v Sharma* [2022] EWHC 612 (Ch) at [49]–[50]: there was no register 9-02
of members but the petitioner was a member by s.112(1) of the Companies Act 2006, by virtue of being the sole subscriber to the company's memorandum of association.

Dispute over locus standi

After the last paragraph, add new paragraphs:

In *Re Compound Photonics* [2019] EWHC 1140 (Ch), an application to strike- 9-07
out the claims of certain petitioners on the basis of lack of standing was dismissed in circumstances where it was arguable that they were registered as members on a proper construction of the register (alternatively, that an application for rectification of the register had realistic prospects) and it made no substantive difference (the issue being whether individuals were registered jointly with a trustee or whether the trustee was the sole registered member).

In *Boston Trust Co Ltd v Verhoef* [2021] EWCA Civ 1176; [2022] B.C.C. 1, it was held that a judge should not have granted permission to continue a double derivative action conditional upon the success of an application to rectify a company's register in order to have standing. Having referred to *Re Starlight Developers Ltd* [2007] B.C.C. 929, it was said that the proper course would have been to stay the application, pending the outcome of the application to rectify the register (by the time, however, the appeal was heard, the register had been rectified and unconditional permission to continue the double derivative claim was granted).

In *Re Motion Pictures Capital Ltd* [2021] EWHC 2504 (Ch); [2022] B.C.C. 62, the petitioner was a member at the time the petition was presented, but his shares were subject to a charge which had become enforceable, whereby the company could transfer the petitioner's shares to itself as his attorney. The board resolved to do so and the petitioner's shares were so transferred. He was removed from the register of members and the respondents sought to strike out the petition. It was held that s.994 required the petitioner to be a member at the time of presentation of the petition, but there was no jurisdictional requirement that he should continue to be a member up until the hearing of the petition. Since it was arguable that the transfer could be impugned, the petitioner still had an interest in pursuing the proceedings and it remained possible that he could obtain the relief which the petition sought, such being a share purchase order (with such other orders as were necessary to restore the position to that which it was prior to the transfer).

PRE-ACTION DISCLOSURE

After the last paragraph, add a new paragraph:

9-08 See *A v B* Unreported, 4 October 2019 at [10]–[11] and *Willow Sports Ltd v SportsLocker24.com Ltd* [2021] EWHC 2524 (Ch) at [15]–[17] as to the effect of the pilot scheme on pre-action disclosure: the jurisdictional requirement that documents sought would fall within standard disclosure is to be approached without regard to the pilot scheme, but the provisions of the pilot scheme should factor into the discretion stage.

PRE-ACTION PROTOCOLS AND THE CHANCERY GUIDE

In the first sentence of the last paragraph, after "respondents, in making", replace "open" with:

9-09 open,

PROCEDURE

Replace list item "(1)" with:

9-10 (1) The petition must be in the prescribed form specifying the grounds and the relief sought.

In order to save time and costs, it is good practice to draft the petition so that it can stand as points of claim.[14] A specimen draft petition, claiming relief on the unfair prejudice ground and winding-up on the just and equitable ground in the alternative, is set out in Appendix 2. It is important for the petitioner's case to be pleaded properly.

A specimen form of Tomlin order in settlement of such a petition is also included in Appendix 2.

In *Bamber v Eaton* [2007] B.C.C. 877, Pumfrey J held that the court had no jurisdiction under CPR r.3.10 to permit an unfair prejudice claim to proceed otherwise than by way of petition as prescribed. See also to the same effect *Goodwin v Cook* (Unreported, 21 June 2018) at [69] and [81] and *In re Osea Road Camp Sites Ltd* [2005] 1 W.L.R. 760 at [15]. But it may be possible to overcome this procedural impediment by the court exercising its wide case management powers, such as requiring the claimant to discontinue the claim and present a petition and directing that all the pleadings in the discontinued claim stand as the pleadings in the petition, with directions to preserve the position as to costs, as was argued in *Boston Trust Co Ltd v Verhoef* (Unreported, 14 October 2022, Mr Ian Karet sitting as a Deputy High Court Judge) at [6]–[8].

[14] See para.9-11. For general observations on the need for particularity in pleadings, which must now be read in the light of CPR Pt 16, see *Re Unisoft Group Ltd (No.2)* [1994] B.C.C. 766 Ch D (Companies Ct); *Re Company (No.007936 of 1994)* [1995] B.C.C. 705 Ch D (Companies Ct); *Re Company (No.002015 of 1996)* [1997] 2 B.C.L.C. 1 Ch D. *Re Kings Solutions Ltd* [2021] EWCA Civ 1943; [2022] B.C.C. 529 at [62]–[67]; *Birkenfield v Denton* [2022] EWHC 436 (Ch) at [82].

At the end of the last paragraph, replace "Vollin Holdings Ltd v Faulkner unreported 11 June 2020 Ch D." with:

Vollin Holdings Ltd v Faulkner [2020] EWHC 1919 (Ch). *Veasey v McDougall* [2022] EWHC 864 (Ch); *Re 99 Hippos Ltd* [2022] EWHC 878 (Ch).

Pleadings

After the quote in the first paragraph, add a new paragraph:

To similar effect, in *Re Kings Solutions Ltd* [2021] EWCA Civ 1943; [2022] B.C.C. 529 it was said at [63], [66]–[67], per Snowden LJ: 9-11

"63. The principle that statements of case should only set out the facts that go to make up each essential element of the cause of action relied upon is particularly relevant to pleadings in unfair prejudice petitions. There has, from the early days of the unfair prejudice jurisdiction, been a clear tendency for petitions and pleadings in such cases to seek to raise myriad grievances and complaints of diverse forms of misconduct against the respondents to the petition. This experience has been especially prevalent in cases in which it is alleged that the company is a quasi-partnership so that equitable considerations are in play. Such wide-ranging allegations are often then said to require extensive disclosure and a lengthy trial at which the entire history of the formation and breakdown of the relationship between the parties is gone through in enormous detail.

66. … Although designed to overcome some of the limitations which beset the oppression remedy under section 210 of the Companies Act 1948, neither section 459 of the Companies Act 1985 nor Section 994 were drafted on the basis that a shareholder could simply complain, for example, that "a course of conduct in relation to the company" had unfairly prejudiced his interests. The potential breadth of what is now Section 994 has been limited and kept within manageable bounds by the express statutory requirements that the acts complained of must either (i) be an act or omission of the company, or (ii) be conduct of the company's affairs rather than acts done in the conduct of a shareholder's personal affairs.

67. Satisfaction of these requirements should not be overlooked or minimised. Petitions and statements of case in unfair prejudice cases should make it clear which limb of Section 994 is being relied upon and should contain a concise statement of the facts upon which the petitioner relies to make out that requirement. On the basis of the majority judgments in *Graham v Every*, it may be legitimate for a concise statement of personal acts of the respondents which are causally connected to an act or omission of the company, or causally connected to conduct of the company's affairs, to be included to support the primary allegation. There is, however, no such justification for allowing other allegations of personal conduct of the respondents, which are not causally connected to an act or omission of the company, or not causally connected to conducting the affairs of the company, to be included in a statement of case under Section 994."

In the first sentence of the second paragraph, after "Re G&G Properties Ltd [2019] EWCA Civ 2046 at", replace "[35]–[39]." with:

[35]–[39]; *Re Kings Solutions Ltd* [2021] EWCA Civ 1943; [2022] B.C.C. 529 at [62]–[67] (cited in part above); *Birkenfield v Denton* [2022] EWHC 436 (Ch) at [82] (and cf. *Financial Technology Ventures II (Q) LP v ETFS Capital Ltd* [2021] JCA 176 at [39]–[47]).

Further information and disclosure

To the end of the last paragraph, before the full stop, add:

9-13 and see now *Broad Idea International Ltd v Convoy Collateral Ltd* [2021] UKPC 24; [2022] 2 W.L.R. 703

Parties to be joined as respondents

After the last paragraph, add a new paragraph:

9-17 In *Re The Hut Group Ltd* [2021] EWCA Civ 904; [2021] B.C.C. 970, the petition sought relief which included an order that the company issue shares so as to redress the allegedly wrongful dilution of the petitioners' shareholding. The Court of Appeal refused to strike out that relief on the basis that this would amount to the expropriation of the property rights of other shareholders who were not joined as respondents to the petition. Any such concern could be addressed by joining the other shareholders, which was a case management issue, with the Court of Appeal endorsing the judge's reliance on *Re Company (No.007281 of 1986)* [1987] B.C.L.C. 593 cited above (and, in any event, the relief sought did not necessarily entail adversely affecting the other shareholders).

Split trials of liability and quantum

Replace the first paragraph with:

9-19 In *Re Annacott Holdings Ltd* [2012] EWCA Civ 998, it was said that generally a split trial of liability and quantum will be ordered: see at [27] of the judgment of Arden LJ. But the overriding objectives of the CPR have the habit of sounding good but being difficult to achieve in practice in complex and weighty litigation, as petitions on the statutory grounds often are. The court is often in the dark as to the real state of the dispute between the parties as disclosed in Pt 36 and other "off the record" offers and negotiations, and in many cases the real dispute between the parties is over value so that the postponement of the determination of that issue is most undesirable, not least because it may well lead to the postponement of the determination of liability for costs (see para.9-27). The concept of unfair prejudice is diffuse and does not easily lend itself to the identification of key issues. The court cannot be expected to wave its magic wand and give the necessary directions of its own motion: it requires the parties to formulate specific proposals, for example, as to the formulation of preliminary issues, for the court's consideration: *Re Rotadata Ltd* [2000] B.C.C. 686 Ch D; [2000] 1 B.C.L.C. 122 (Companies Ct); see also now the *Chancery Guide* (2022), paras 6-10 to 6-16, requiring parties to consider matters such as a split trial or preliminary issues at the earliest opportunity (in advance of the first CMC/CMCC) and to formulate carefully any such proposals, including as to whether they would genuinely assist the efficient case management of the proceedings. There is much to be said in many cases in this area of the law, in terms of cost-effectiveness, speed, the reasonable expectations of the parties, the prospect of appeals, and pressure to reach a final settlement without a trial, for the "old-fashioned" idea of a single trial of all the live issues, including valuation and/or quantum: *Electrical Waste Recycling v City Electrical Factors* [2012] EWHC 38 (Ch); *Roadchef (Employees Benefits Trustees) Ltd v Ingram Hill* [2013] EWHC 939 (Ch); and see para.9-20. The real issue between the parties, although this will usually be hidden from the court behind the veil of "without prejudice" communications, is likely to relate to valuation and the longer the determination of that issue is postponed, the longer the dispute, including in particular the dispute over entitlement to costs, will last, to the detriment of the party with the fewer resources.[27] It is very easy for a party resisting a single trial of all the issues to assert that this will save costs, when the opposite is its real motivation. See also para.9-10. Hence, it is thought that the court has jurisdiction from an early stage to direct[28] a binding valuation of the company and the shares to be purchased, a reversal of the idea of a split trial of liability and quantum. Yet against such a course must be weighed the dangers of the determination of preliminary issues: see para.9-20.

[27] It is therefore a useful step in the right direction that the parties are now routinely ordered to exchange non-binding share valuations at an early stage: see para.9-10.

[28] The costs of a full-blown valuation by the court, with experts instructed by both sides and cross-examined at length, are notoriously burdensome.

After the last paragraph, add a new paragraph:

In *Re Compound Photonics* [2019] EWHC 1140 (Ch) at [30]–[34], a split trial was ordered where the facts to be found at liability were considered likely to affect valuation.

STRIKE-OUT AND SUMMARY JUDGMENT

To the end of the last paragraph, add:

Cf. *Re Electrical Control Installations Ltd* [2021] EWHC 2661 (Ch); [2022] B.C.C. 199: a settlement agreement releasing all claims relating to a "dispute" (concerning payments of dividends) and "all other claims relating to ... [a] shareholding in [the company], which are known or reasonably ought to be known ... as of the date of [the agreement]", was held to be apt to comprehend allegations of unfair prejudice (although not those of which the petitioner was unaware and of which he had no reason to know at the time of the settlement); the court rejected a submission that a petition under ss.994–996 was not a "claim" for such purposes. **9-23**

After the last paragraph, add new a paragraph:

In *Re Hut Group Ltd* [2021] EWCA Civ 904; [2021] B.C.C. 970, large parts of the petition were struck out, including as to allegations of bad faith/improper purpose in the dilution of petitioner's shareholding in the absence of allegations pleaded which were capable of establishing bad faith/improper purpose.

Abuse of process

After the paragraph, add new paragraphs:

Conversely, it may be an abuse of process to attempt to use insolvency proceedings to forestall an unfair prejudice petition: *Jones v Sky Wheels Group Ltd* [2020] EWHC 1112 (Ch); [2020] B.P.I.R. 851; *Motion Capital Ltd v Clarance* [2021] EWHC 2504 (Ch); [2021] 6 WLUK 321. **9-25**

In *Re Compound Photonics Group Ltd* [2020] EWHC 3176 (Ch); [2021] B.C.C. 249, the petitioners alleged that the respondents had wrongfully excluded them from the management of the business in breach of the shareholders' agreement and articles. The respondents defended the petition on the basis that the petitioners had been negligent in the management of the business in breach of the same agreement, and counterclaimed for very substantial damages. Shortly before trial, the respondents abandoned the counterclaim. The petitioners' application to debar the respondents from defending the petition failed, it being held that the respondents' conduct in maintaining an intimidatory counterclaim until the last minute did not amount to an abuse of process. Having referred to *Summers v Fairclough Homes Ltd* [2012] UKSC 26; [2012] 1 W.L.R. 2004 and *Alpha Rocks Solicitors v Alade* [2015] EWCA Civ 685; [2015] 1 W.L.R. 4534, it was said that this was a case where there could still be a fair trial.

Taylor Goodchild Ltd v Taylor [2021] EWCA Civ 1135; [2022] 2 B.C.L.C. 27 concerned a company, a solicitors' practice, equally owned by two solicitors, T and G, who practiced through it. After an agreement in principle that they should part their ways, but before any formal agreement to that effect, T set up a new company and diverted work to it. By a s.994 petition, G obtained an order that T sell his shares to G, on the basis that T had breached his duties as a director. After the share purchase, the company (now owned wholly by G) bought proceedings against T for (i) repayment of monies outstanding on his director's loan account; (ii) against T's new company for sums which it had received in respect of work-in-progress owed to the original company; and (iii) against both T and the new company for an account of profits for work which the new company carried out while T remained a director of the old company and work on files which T had taken. At first instance, the claims other than that relating to the loan account were held to be a *Henderson v Henderson* type abuse of process: it was relief which could have been sought in the unfair prejudice petition and the petitioner had given no notice of the possibility that such a future claim might be given as per the guidance in *Aldi Stores Ltd v WSP Group Plc* [2007] EWCA Civ 1260; [2008] 1 W.L.R. 748. The Court of Appeal held that the subsequent proceedings were not an abuse, placing particular emphasis on the point that while claims against T and his new company could have been brought within an unfair prejudice petition, it was not a straightforward question as to whether they should have been, having regard to the observations in, e.g. *Re Chime Corp Ltd* (2004) 7 HJFCAR 546 as to claims which should more properly be brought by derivative action (see para.7-60).

COSTS

Success

Replace footnote 32 with:

9-26 [32] For reviews of the authorities and applicable principles, see *Amin v Amin (Costs)* [2010] EWHC 827 (Ch) and *Re Southern Counties Fresh Foods Ltd* [2011] 3 Costs L.O. 343; *Re Sprintroom Ltd* [2021] EWHC 960 (Ch). See *Hunt v Aziz* [2012] 1 W.L.R. 317 as to the undesirability of pre-empting the trial judge's discretion as to costs.

Offers

At the end of the first paragraph, before the full stop, add:

9-27 ; *Re Sprintroom Ltd* [2021] EWHC 960 (Ch)

After the last paragraph, add a new paragraph:

In *Langer v McKeown* [2021] EWCA Civ 1792; [2022] 1 W.L.R. 1255, however, it was held that a judge was entitled to make an order for costs after the liability trial in circumstances where a "without prejudice save as to costs" offer had been made. Such offers were not to be treated as the same as offers under CPR Pt 36. Moreover, there was no principle that the Court should not make an order for costs up to the date of any offer (whether under CPR Pt 36 or not) following success at the liability trial. And the Court may still exceptionally, even where an offer under CPR Pt 36 has been made, make an order for costs on an issue-by-issue basis and not defer the question of costs to the quantum trial.

Success on some, failure on other issues

To the end of the first paragraph, add:

See *Re Sprintroom Ltd* [2021] EWHC 960 (Ch) for an example of a petitioner being awarded a percentage of his costs to reflect, among other things, lack of success on some issues. **9-29**

PARTICIPATION BY COMPANY—USE OF COMPANY FUNDS

In the fourth sentence of the second paragraph, after "this area (at", replace "155h–156c):" with:

333A–333G): **9-34**

Replace the end of the last sentence of the last paragraph after "minority shareholder to enforce the terms of a" with:

shareholders' agreement: discussed in Ch.6, para.6-40. See also *JAB Nominees (Aust) Pty Ltd v Auswild* [2020] VSC 731 at [232]–[241] in which the general principle was affirmed that directors must be entitled to authorise a company to expend its own funds to bring claims against third parties, even if those parties happen to number among the company's own shareholders; but, on the particular facts, the proceedings brought by the company were so closely connected with a plan to acquire those shareholders' shares as to constitute oppression, which justified an order that the directors authorising the proceedings by the company should reimburse the company for those costs.

After the last paragraph, add new paragraphs:

See *Koza Ltd v Koza Altin Isletmeleri AS* [2021] EWHC 786 (Ch) at [64]–[77] for a review and summary of the principles as to costs expenditure by the company, concluding at [66] that, whatever the procedural context, if the real contest is between parties other than the company itself, it will be a misfeasance for the company's directors to cause its funds to be expended on the legal costs of that contest. On an application to restrain the company from incurring costs, *American Cyanamid* principles were applied.

Cf. *Hashmi v Lorimer-Wing* [2022] EWHC 191 (Ch); [2022] B.C.C. 687 in which the company's counterclaim to an unfair prejudice petition which alleged breaches of the petitioner's director's duties and contract was struck out as the company, bringing the proceedings on the authority of the sole remaining director, had not discharged the onus of showing "not merely that the board's decision to participate could have been, but that it was, arrived at by an honest and reasonable board properly looking to what was necessary or expedient in the interests of the company as a whole." as described in *Re Company (No.001126 of 1992)* [1993] B.C.C. 325 at 334E. The Court, however, refused to grant an injunction restraining the company from expending funds on further participation, noting among other things, that there were matters on which the company could properly expend funds, such as disclosure.

See also *King v Kings Solutions Group Ltd* [2022] EWHC 1099 (Ch) at [53]–[56], for a summary of the principles as to company participation.

CHAPTER 10

Winding-up on the Just and Equitable Ground

TABLE OF CONTENTS

PARALLEL WITH UNFAIR PREJUDICE REMEDY

At the end of the first paragraph, replace "Re Paramount Powders (UK) Ltd [2019] EWCA Civ 1644 at [47]." with:

Re Paramount Powders (UK) Ltd [2019] EWCA Civ 1644; [2020] B.C.C. 152 at [47]. Cf. *Financial Technology Ventures II (Q) LP v ETFS Capital Ltd* [2021] JCA 176 at [268]. **10-03**

GROUNDS FOR WINDING-UP ON JUST AND EQUITABLE BASIS

General principle

After the last paragraph, add new paragraphs:

The just-and-equitable winding-up jurisdiction was examined by the Privy Council in *Chu v Lau* [2020] UKPC 24; [2020] 1 W.L.R. 4656. L and C were equal shareholders in OSL, of which PBM was a wholly owned subsidiary. L and C were also the sole directors of both OSL and PBM. The trial judge found OSL to be a quasi-partnership. PBM had a 49% shareholding in a joint venture company with a state-owned entity of the PRC. The relationship between L and C broke down. The trial judge found that OSL (and PBM) was in a hopeless state of functional deadlock, that L and C had suffered an irretrievable breakdown and all trust and confidence had gone. He ordered a winding-up. The Eastern Caribbean Court of Appeal reversed the judge and discharged the winding-up order, identifying four errors said to have been made by the judge: (a) he had wrongly taken into account **10-09** dissent at the level of the joint venture company rather than OSL; (b) he had wrongly focused on deadlock as at the commencement of the proceedings, rather than at trial; (c) he had failed to take into account that both L and C were free to sell their shares as a means of avoiding deadlock; and (d) he had failed to consider alternative remedies such as a buy-out before ordering a winding-up. The Privy Council restored the judge's order. The Privy Council, with Lord Briggs giving the majority judgment, distinguished between deadlock cases, which could found a just-and-equitable winding-up order irrespective of whether the company was a quasi-partnership, and breakdown of trust and confidence, which of itself could be sufficient to justify a just-and-equitable winding-up order in the case of a quasi-partnership: see further para.10-17. The judge's findings as to matters at the level of the joint venture company did rightly go to the question of breakdown of trust and confidence (and also were relevant to deadlock). Lady Arden, in an assenting additional judgment, would also have found that a just-and-equitable order was justified by C's practical exclusion of L from participation in management. The judge was correct to take into account the position as at trial (and in any event had made sufficient findings as to the position when the proceedings were commenced). There was little to suggest that L could have sold his shares to a third party. The onus was on the respondent to establish that there was a satisfactory remedy falling short of a winding-up order and the judge had given cogent reasons why none of those suggested offered a realistic alternative to winding-up.

See now also *Financial Technology Ventures II (Q) LP v ETFS Capital Ltd* [2021] JCA 176 at [267]–[274] for a summary of the applicable principles upon which a court may, but is not bound, to make a winding up order on the just and equitable basis.

Prejudice

After "which they complain:", replace "Re Paramount Powders (UK) Ltd [2019] EWCA Civ 1644" with:

10-10 *Re Paramount Powders (UK) Ltd* [2019] EWCA Civ 1644; [2020] B.C.C. 152

Categorisation

(1) Loss of substratum

Replace footnote 33 with:

10-12 [33] *Citco Global Custody v Y2K Finance Inc* unreported 25 November 2009 per Bannister QC J; *Aris Multi–Strategy Lending Fund Ltd v Quantek Opportunity Fund Ltd* unreported 15 December 2010 (BVI) per Bannister J. But see now *Delco Participation BV v Green Elite Ltd* BVIHCVAPP 2017/129 Unreported 15 June 2018, in which the Eastern Caribbean Court of Appeal, reversing the first instance decision, made a winding-up order on the just-and-equitable ground in respect of a company whose sole purpose was to hold shares in another company on the basis of loss of substratum after those shares had been sold and the argument that there was a continuing ancillary function of dealing with the proceeds of sale could not displace the point that the main object could no longer be carried out, such that just and equitable winding-up was appropriate.

After the last paragraph, add new paragraphs:

In *Re Klimvest Plc* [2022] EWHC 596 (Ch); [2022] B.C.C. 747, three individuals (ED, FS and MB) had set up a business to develop and distribute certain software written by ED and FS in 1995. Various entities were formed for the business. The company subject to the proceedings was formed in 2002 and in due course became the effective holding company for the business. It also acquired other companies in the software field. In 2004, an outside investor acquired shares in a capital-raising exercise. The company was listed in 2006, and some other outside investors acquired shares. ED became unhappy with aspects of the management from 2013 onwards and ceased to be employed by the company, but remained a director for the time being. In 2019, the business was sold by an asset sale. Contrary to ED and FS' assumption, however, the company was not liquidated and the proceeds of sale not distributed to the shareholders. Rather, MB who had acquired an effective majority shareholding defeated a resolution to have the company enter into members' voluntary liquidation and passed a resolution "to approve the investment strategy of investing in promising technology companies". ED was required to submit himself for re-election as a director pursuant to the articles and was not re-elected.

Following a review of the authorities as to just-and-equitable winding-up on the basis of loss of substratum at [214]–[225], at [2264]–[228], HHJ Mark Cawson QC (sitting as a Judge of the High Court) concluded:

> "226. In seeking to reconcile the various authorities identified above, it is necessary, in my judgment, to focus upon why loss of substratum ought to provide a basis for a contributory to seek to wind up a company. As to this, it is important to bear firmly in mind Lord Parker's observation in *Cotman v Brougham* (supra) at 520 that the question is fundamentally one of equity between the company and its shareholders.
>
> 227. I consider that particular insight in the circumstances of the present case is provided by the reasoning as to why loss of substratum or purpose might prove a basis for winding up on the just and equitable ground as explained by Jenkins J (later Lord Jenkins) in *Re Eastern Telegraph Co., Ltd.* [1947] 2 All ER 104. At 109F, he quoted with approval the first paragraph of the headnote to the report of the judgment of the Court of Appeal in *Re Haven Gold Mining Company* (1882) 20 Ch.D. 151, namely:
>
> 'Where the court is satisfied that the subject-matter of the business for which a company was formed has substantially ceased to exist, it will make an order for winding up the company, although the large majority of the shareholders desire to continue to carry on the company.'
>
> Jenkins J then continued:
>
> 'That, I take it, means that, if a shareholder has invested his money in the shares of the company on the footing that it is going to carry out some particular object, he cannot be forced against his will by the votes of his fellow shareholders to continue to adventure his money on some quite different project or speculation.'
>
> 228. This, in my judgment, amply supports the proposition that, on appropriate facts, it may be just and equitable to wind up a company if its directors cause it to embark upon acts which are outside and different from what can fairly be regarded as having been within the general intention and common understanding of the members when they became members, even though the company could still pursue its original objects as set out in its memorandum of association, a conclusion supported by the decision of Menhennitt J in the Australian case of *Re Tivoli Freeholds Ltd* [1972] VR 445, at 469 (Supreme Court of Victoria)."

In concluding that there had been a loss of substratum, the judge summarised his reasons as follows:

> "245. I reach this conclusion for a number of reasons:
>
> i) Firstly, I consider that it can properly be said that it is now impossible, or at least practically impossible, for the Company to pursue its main or paramount object or purpose as identified above given the sale of the Company's assets and the particular nature of the business of the Company,

even if the main or paramount purpose is best expressed in the terms of the 'principal activities' referred to in the accounts for the year ended 31 December 2018 [viz. 'to develop and distribute productivity software for training, support and translation of or on ERP applications such as Oracle or SAP, and to deliver related consultancy services' [237]]. As matters stand, having regard to the nature of the business and the fact of the sale, let alone ED's exclusion and MB's control of the Company, it would be practically impossible to recreate a like business so as to pursue the main or paramount object or purpose previously pursued.

ii) Secondly, even if that is not right, and the pursuit of the Company's main or paramount object or purpose is still practically possible, the sale of the assets of the Company to P1C taken together with what is now proposed with regard to investing in promising technology companies, given the very different nature of the venture that is now proposed, represents, as I see it, a clear abandonment of the pre-existing main or paramount object or purpose of the Company such that it is just and equitable that the Company be wound up.

iii) Thirdly, even if the above analysis is incorrect, I consider that the difference between the Company actively carrying on its own business through subsidiaries that it controls, with the main or paramount object or purpose referred to above, and what is now proposed by way of a company under MB's direction making investments at his discretion in promising technology companies, represents the carrying on of such a fundamentally different activity to that carried on prior to the sale in January 2019, that one can only but conclude that the Company proposes to embark upon a course of conduct so fundamentally outside or different from what can fairly be regarded as having been within the general intention or common understanding of the members of the Company when they became members, that, subject to the existence of any alternative remedy and other discretionary considerations, it would be unjust and inequitable to require them, against their will, to continue to invest in the quite different and speculative venture that is proposed, and therefore just and equitable that the Company be wound up."

See now also *Financial Technology Ventures II (Q) LP v ETFS Capital Ltd* [2021] JCA 176 at [267]–[274] for a summary of the applicable principles in the case of a change of the nature of business.

(2) Deadlock

Replace footnote 34 with:

10-13 [34] In *Re Davis Investments (East Ham) Ltd* [1961] 1 W.L.R. 1396 CA at 1399, Donovan LJ said: "Mr Finer's argument goes to this length: that in a case of a two man company, if the shareholders, being equal in their shareholding, fall out, one of them alleging that further co-operation is impossible, then the court, in the absence of a reply from the other shareholder, must at once treat them as though they were partners and order a winding up, as it would, in a partnership case, order a dissolution. I do not think that is the law."

(3) Justifiable loss of confidence due to mismanagement

After the quote in the fourth paragraph, add new paragraphs:

10-14 In *Ninotre Investment Ltd v Strong Light Investments Ltd* [2021] HKCFI 3095, a winding-up order was made in respect of a solvent Cayman company listed on the Hong Kong stock exchange, of which the petitioners held 3% and the respondents around 44%. This was on the basis of serial misconduct by the Board which was populated by the respondents' proxies. The Court recognised the exceptionality of the remedy but considered that nothing short of a winding-up order was sufficient in the face of such misconduct.

In *Financial Technology Ventures II (Q) LP v ETFS Capital Ltd* [2021] JCA 176 at [272] it was noted that the availability of a winding-up order on this basis was not dependent on establishing a quasi-partnership. Further, it did not require establishing an actionable breach of fiduciary duty or dishonesty.

(5) Breakdown of trust and confidence

In the second sentence of the second paragraph, replace "Re Paramount Powders (UK) Ltd [2019] EWCA Civ 1644" with:

Re Paramount Powders (UK) Ltd [2019] EWCA Civ 1644; 2020] B.C.C. 152 **10-17**

After the last paragraph, add new paragraphs:

In *Chu v Lau* [2020] UKPC 24; [2020] 1 W.L.R. 4656, it was held that a breakdown in trust and confidence in a quasi-partnership was a ground upon which a winding up order might be made. Lord Briggs said:

"14. A just and equitable winding-up may be ordered where the company's members have fallen out in two related but distinct situations, which may or may not overlap. First, a winding-up may be ordered to resolve what may conveniently be labelled a functional deadlock. This is where an inability of members to co-operate in the management of the company's affairs leads to an inability of the company to function at board or shareholder level. Functional deadlock of this paralysing kind was first clearly recognised as a ground for a just and equitable winding-up by Vaughan Williams J in *In re Sailing Ship Kentmere Co* [1897] WN 58, a decision on the jurisdiction conferred by section 79 of the (UK) Companies Act 1862 (25 & 26 Vict, c 89).

15. Secondly, where the company is a corporate quasi-partnership, an irretrievable breakdown in trust and confidence between the participating members may justify a just and equitable winding-up, essentially on the same grounds as would justify the dissolution of a true partnership. This jurisprudence was developed as an aspect of the law of partnership in England in the mid-19th Century, and is exemplified in the following passage from the judgment of Sir John Romilly MR in *Harrison v Tennant* (1856) 21 Beav 482, at 496–497: 'I do not base my decision upon any particular reported case, but upon the principle that the circumstances under which the parties entered into the partnership have, by matters over which they have no control, materially altered, that these altered circumstances have, combined with the conduct of the parties themselves, produced a mistrust which the Court cannot say is unreasonable; and that, taking all these things together, it is impossible that the partnership can be conducted upon the footing on which it was originally contemplated, without injury to all these persons concerned, and that taking all these matters together, it makes this a case in which, in my opinion, it is the duty of the Court to pronounce a decree for the dissolution of the partnership.' It is clear, for example from *Pease v Hewitt* (1862) 31 Beav 22 and *Atwood v Maude* (1868) LR 3 Ch App 369, at p 373, that a dissolution of a partnership might be ordered even where both parties were to blame for the breakdown in mutual trust and confidence.

16. This ground for the dissolution of a partnership was developed as the basis for the just and equitable winding-up of a company in the UK in the early 20th century, where the relationship between the members approximated to that of partners. Page 7 Landmark cases include *Symington v Symingtons' Quarries Ltd* (1905) 8 F 121, a decision of the Scottish Court of Session, and in *In re Yenidje Tobacco Company Ltd* [1916] 2 Ch 426, a decision of the English Court of Appeal. In the latter case, at p 432, speaking of two businessmen holding equal shares in the company who had spectacularly fallen out, Lord Cozens-Hardy

> MR said: 'If ever there was a case of deadlock I think it exists here; but, whether it exists or not, I think the circumstances are such that we ought to apply, if necessary, the analogy of the partnership law and to say that this company is now in a state which could not have been contemplated by the parties when the company was formed and which ought to be terminated as soon as possible.'
>
> 17. The important potential distinction between the two types of breakdown case is this. If there is a complete functional deadlock, then a winding-up may be ordered regardless whether the company is a corporate quasi-partnership. But if the company is of that type, then a breakdown of trust and confidence may justify a winding-up even where there may not be a complete functional deadlock. In the former case winding-up is a remedy for paralysis. In the latter it is the response of equity to a state of affairs between individuals who agreed to work together on the basis of mutual trust and confidence where that trust and confidence has completely gone. But of course both may exist together, and a complete breakdown in trust and confidence may well be the cause of functional deadlock, in a two party quasi-partnership like the present."

In *Il v Yesilkaya* [2021] EWHC 1695 (Ch), the Court declined to make an order for winding-up on the just-and-equitable basis in the case of an established breakdown of trust and confidence attributable to both quasi-partners in a quasi-partnership, having regard to the misconduct of the petitioner, particularly his seeking to strip the business and deceiving his quasi-partner.

In *Loveridge v Loveridge* [2021] EWCA Civ 1697; [2022] B.C.C. 324, Falk J (with whom the full panel agreed) took from *O'Neill v Phillips* [1999] 1 W.L.R. 1092; [1999] 2 All E.R. 961 at 1104–1105 that

> "[117] ... a breakdown in relations, including where there has been a loss of trust and confidence, is not sufficient to found an unfair prejudice petition where (as on the facts of that case) there has been no exclusion from management. There was no right to exit 'at will' where trust and confidence has broken down. Lord Hoffmann also doubted whether a dissolution would even be granted under partnership law if there was no exclusion from management and the business could be continued."

Falk J went on to observe at [140] when considering just-and-equitable winding-up that a "a simple breakdown in relations is not sufficient" (referring to Floyd LJ's dictum at [64] in the earlier hearing in the Court of Appeal in the same case, *Loveridge v Loveridge* [2020] EWCA Civ 1104). Falk J continued at [146]:

> "It is clear from the judgments of Lord Wilberforce and Lord Cross in *Westbourne Galleries* that it is not a prerequisite of a winding up order on the just and equitable ground that there is a deadlock affecting the operation of the business, or that the conduct of those opposing the order should have been unjust or inequitable. In a quasi-partnership case a winding up may be ordered where there has been a complete breakdown of trust and confidence of a kind that would have justified dissolution of a partnership (see for example the judgment of Lord Cross at pp.383-4). For a recent discussion of this see Lord Briggs' judgment in *Lau v Chu* [2020] UKPC 24; [2020] 1 W.L.R. 4656 at [15]-[19]. However, whilst such a breakdown is a relevant factor it is not by itself determinative. The test remains whether it is just and equitable to order a winding up. This is illustrated by a recent Court of Appeal decision, *Re Paramount Powders (UK) Ltd* [2019] EWCA Civ 1644; [2020] B.C.C. 152. In that case there was a breakdown of trust and confidence between brothers in a quasi-partnership, but the petitioner failed in a winding up petition in circumstances where the situation was attributable to his own misconduct. I would respectfully agree that a breakdown of trust and confidence cannot of itself be determinative. If it were otherwise, what is generally regarded as the exceptional remedy of winding up

would offer a route to the sort of "no-fault divorce" that Lord Hoffmann concluded was not available."

DISCRETION

At the end of the paragraph, after "333 at [46]", add:
; *Il v Yesilkaya* [2021] EWHC 1695 (Ch) **10-18**

COLLATERAL PURPOSE AND ALTERNATIVE REMEDIES GENERALLY

After the last paragraph, add new paragraphs:

In *Chu v Lau* [2020] UKPC 24; [2020] 1 W.L.R. 4656 at [20]–[21], it was held that the burden of proof is on the petitioner to show that winding-up would be just and equitable absent consideration of other remedies; the legal burden of proof then shifts to the respondent to prove that the petitioner has unreasonably failed to pursue some other remedy. **10-23**

In *Ninotre Investment Ltd v Strong Light Investments Ltd* [2021] HKCFI 3095, a winding-up order was made in respect of a solvent Cayman company listed on the Hong Kong stock exchange, of which the petitioners held 3% and the respondents around 44%. This was on the basis of serial misconduct by the board which was populated by the respondents' proxies. The Court recognised the exceptionality of the remedy but considered that nothing short of a winding-up order was sufficient in the face of such misconduct.

CHAPTER 11

Personal Rights of Shareholders

TABLE OF CONTENTS

THE SHAREHOLDER'S LOSS—THE RULE AGAINST REFLECTIVE LOSS

At the end of the penultimate paragraph, replace "Sevilleja v Marex Financial Ltd [2020] UKSC 31." with:

Sevilleja v Marex Financial Ltd [2020] UKSC 31; [2021] A.C. 309. **11-06**

Replace footnote 4 with:

[4] *Marex* [2020] UKSC 31 at [51]–[52]; Lord Hodge called it the Court of Appeal's "articulation" of the rule in *Foss v Harbottle*: at [102]. The rule in *Prudential* has been applied in a number of cases: *Humberclyde Finance Group Ltd v Hicks* unreported 4 November 2001 Ch D (Neuberger J); *Day v Cook* [2003] B.C.C. 256; *Shaker v Al-Bedrawi* [2003] Ch. 350; *Ellis v Property Leeds (UK) Ltd* [2002] 2 B.C.L.C. 175; *Malhotra v Malhotra* [2015] 1 B.C.L.C. 428 at [53]–[63]; *Barclay Pharmaceuticals Ltd v Waypharm LP* [2013] 2 B.C.L.C. 551; *International Leisure Ltd v First National Trustee Co UK Ltd* [2013] Ch. 346; *Sivagnanam v Barclays Bank Plc* [2015] EWHC 3985 (Comm); *Re Hut Group Ltd* [2020] EWHC 5 (Ch) and [2021] EWCA Civ 904; [2021] B.C.C. 970. **11-08**

After the last paragraph, add new paragraphs:

The reflective loss rule as explained in *Marex* fell for further consideration in *Primeo Fund (in official liquidation) v Bank of Bermuda (Cayman) Ltd* [2021] UKPC 22; [2021] B.C.C. 1015. Primeo, an investment fund, made investments in BLMIS, the vehicle for Mr Madoff's Ponzi scheme. It did so, both directly and also indirectly (through two feeder funds, Herald and Alpha—i.e. Primeo provided funds to Herald and Alpha in return for shares in those companies, with Herald and Alpha investing those funds in BLMIS). Then, later, Primeo restructured its investments such that all of its previously direct investments in BLMIS were transferred to Herald in return for new shares in Herald. Primeo claimed against R1 and R2. R2, for practical purposes, was administrator and custodian of Primeo either by direct agreement with Primeo, or by delegation from the first respondent (R1). R2 was also administrator and custodian for Herald (but R1 had no relationship with Herald) and sub-administrator for Alpha: thus, Herald (and Alpha) also brought claims against R2 as respects the same investments. The Privy Council held that Primeo's claims as respects its direct investments were not barred by the reflective loss principle, since the critical question was the characterisation of those claims at the time which they arose: they were Primeo's own claims, not claims by Primeo as a shareholder of Herald. The fact that, by the time proceedings were brought, Primeo held those investments through Herald did not alter that. The fact that were Herald to make a full recovery against R2, that would in effect cure Primeo's loss, did not mean that the reflective loss rule was engaged, but rather was to be managed as an issue of potential double recovery. Lord Kitchin and Lord Sales, delivering the judgment of the board, reasoned:

> "50. Lord Reed (para 79) [in *Marex*] distinguished two types of case:
>
> > '... (1) cases where claims are brought by a shareholder in respect of loss which he has suffered in that capacity, in the form of a diminution in share value or in distributions, which is the consequence of loss sustained by the company, in respect of which the company has a cause of action against the same wrongdoer, and (2) cases where claims are brought, whether by a shareholder or by anyone else, in respect of loss which does not fall within that description, but where the company has a right of action in respect of substantially the same loss.'
>
> In the first type of case, the reflective loss rule applies and the shareholder is barred from seeking recovery for loss they may have suffered. In the second type of case, the reflective loss rule has no application and the claimant can sue for loss they have suffered, even though they happen also to be a shareholder in a company which has a cause of action against the same wrongdoer. Lord Hodge (para 98) stated the position in similar terms: '[the rule excluding recovery] ... relates only to the diminution in value of shares or in distributions which the shareholder suffers in his capacity as a shareholder as a result of the company having itself suffered actionable damage. When a shareholder pursues a personal claim against a wrongdoer in another capacity ... the exclusion has no application'.
>
> 51. The present hearing is concerned with identifying where the boundary lies between these two types of case. It is helpful to focus first on Primeo's claims in respect of its direct investments in BLMIS. Primeo submits that its claims against R1 and R2 for losses in respect of its direct investments fall within the second category, and that the reflective loss rule has no application. R1 and R2 submit that Primeo's claims fall within the first category and that the judge and the Court of Appeal were therefore right to hold that Primeo is barred by the reflective loss rule from recovery for its losses.
>
> 52. In *Marex*, the Supreme Court was concerned to ensure that the reflective loss rule was kept within proper bounds and given limited scope. Lord Reed and Lord Hodge explain the ambit of the rule as limited to cases where a claimant suffers loss in its capacity as shareholder in a company through a diminution in the value of its shares in that company, ie through the mechanism of a wrong done to that company which has a knock-on effect on the value of the shares held by the shareholder. They explain the justification for the rule, as derived from the principle in *Foss v Harbottle*, as based on the fact that by becoming a member of the company the shareholder agrees to 'follow the fortunes of the company' in relation to losses suffered by it as a result of wrongs done to the company and agrees that the company's organs will have the right to decide whether claims should or should not be brought in respect of such wrongs (see paras 35 and 37 per Lord Reed and paras 99 and 108 per Lord Hodge). As Lord Reed said (para 81), 'the effect of the rule in *Foss v Harbottle* is that the shareholder has entrusted the management of the company's right of action to its decision- making organs, including, ultimately, the majority of members voting in general meeting.' Lord Hodge said (para 100), '[the reflective loss rule] is a rule of company law arising from the nature of the shareholder's investment and participation in a limited company and excludes a shareholder's claim made in its capacity as shareholder.'

53. In the Board's judgment, on proper application of the reasoning of Lord Reed and Lord Hodge in *Marex*, the reflective loss rule has no application to bar Primeo from claiming in respect of the losses it suffered each time it made a direct investment in BLMIS, nor from claiming in respect of the losses it maintains it suffered by loss of the chance to redeem its BLMIS investments down to the time of the Herald Transfer. In the Board's view, those losses were not suffered by Primeo 'in its capacity as shareholder' of Herald. So far as is relevant, at the time Primeo suffered such losses it was not a shareholder in Herald. This point is not affected by the fact that in the period up to 1 May 2007 Primeo also held some indirect investments in BLMIS via Primeo's ownership of shares in Herald; those investments were completely separate from Primeo's direct investments with which the Board is concerned at this point in this judgment.

...

55. ... It is important to note that the reflective loss rule is, as was made clear in the majority judgments in *Marex*, a rule of substantive law associated with the rule in Foss v Harbottle and concerned with the recognition in law of particular types of loss. It is not a procedural rule concerned only with the avoidance of double recovery.

56. As Mr Smith submitted, according to the analysis of the majority in *Marex* the focus is on the nature of the loss, which involves consideration of the capacity in which the claimant suffered the loss and the form of the loss (ie whether it was suffered as a diminution in the value of shares held by the claimant or as a reduction in the dividends payable to them). The issue is one of the characterisation of the loss, which depends upon its status (that is, whether it is recognised or not by the law) at the time it is suffered. The test of whether the substantive rule is engaged or not in relation to a cause of action which arises as property in the hands of a person is to look at the nature of the loss at that time: see *Marex*, paras 79 and 89 per Lord Reed."

As respects the indirect investments, although the losses were suffered by Primeo as a shareholder and the losses consisted of diminution in value, the claim was held to be not precluded by the reflective loss rule on the more narrow basis that the "common wrongdoer" requirement was not satisfied.

For the need to show that the company had suffered reflective loss in order to maintain a derivative claim, see para.6-07.

A CAUSE OF ACTION VESTED IN THE SHAREHOLDER

A common law duty of care

After the second sentence of the first paragraph, after "but this is not conclusive.", add:

This is an area of the law which has seen much recent development, culminating in the recent decision of the Supreme Court in *Manchester Building Society v Grant Thornton UK LLP* [2021] UKSC 20; [2022] A.C. 783 referred to below. **11-09**

Replace footnote 8 with:

8 For a case where the test of assumption of responsibility was held to be less appropriate than the proximity of the relationship, see *Customs and Excise Commissioners v Barclays Bank Plc* [2007] 1 A.C. 181 (bank affected by freezing injunction owed no duty of care to beneficiary; no relationship "equivalent to contract"). Cf. *Royal Bank of Scotland International Ltd v JP SPC 4* [2022] UKPC 18; [2022] P.N.L.R. 22 (the duty owed by a bank to refrain from executing a customer's order if the bank has reasonable grounds for believing that the order is an attempt to defraud the customer, established *Barclays Bank Plc v Quincecare Ltd* [1992] 4 All E.R. 363, is not owed to third parties).

After the last paragraph, add new paragraphs:

Manchester Building Society v Grant Thornton UK LLP [2021] UKSC 20; [2022] A.C. 783 now sets out a fundamental re-statement of the law of the scope of a duty of care in the case of the provision of advice and information, as also reflected in the judgment in *Khan v Meadows* [2021] UKSC 21; [2022] A.C. 852 handed down on the same day. In the *Grant Thornton* case, the building society had been negligently advised by its auditor that it could apply hedge accounting to certain interest rate swaps. Relying on that advice, the building society entered into long-term interest rate swaps. The hedge accounting hid what became a severe mismatch between the negative value of the swaps and the mortgage loans. When the auditor realised its error, the building society had to restate its accounts to show reduced assets and insufficient regulatory capital. The building society had to close out the swaps, paying substantial mark-to-market losses. The question was whether the building society could recover those losses against the auditor. In allowing the appeal, and holding that those losses were recoverable (although subject to a reduction for contributory negligence), the majority summarised the principles at [4]:

> "4. … (i) the scope of duty question should be located within a general conceptual framework in the law of the tort of negligence; (ii) the scope of the duty of care assumed by a professional adviser is governed by the purpose of the duty, judged on an objective basis by reference to the purpose for which the advice is being given (in the context of this judgment, we use the expression 'purpose of the duty' in this sense); (iii) in line with the judgment of Lord Sumption JSC in *Hughes-Holland* at paras 39–44, the distinction between 'advice' cases and 'information' cases drawn by Lord Hoffmann in his speech in *SAAMCO* should not be treated as a rigid straitjacket; and, following on from this, (iv) counterfactual analysis of the kind proposed by Lord Hoffmann in SAAMCO should be regarded only as a tool to cross-check the result given pursuant to analysis of the purpose of the duty at (ii), but one which is subordinate to that analysis and which should not supplant or subsume it. The points which we make below in relation to the facts of the case as found by the judge reflect our view regarding the proper approach to be adopted …".

Further in "locating the scope of duty question", the majority formulated a series of six questions which arose in a negligence claim:

> 6. …
> (1) Is the harm (loss, injury and damage) which is the subject matter of the claim actionable in negligence? (the actionability question)
> (2) What are the risks of harm to the claimant against which the law imposes on the defendant a duty to take care? (the scope of duty question)
> (3) Did the defendant breach his or her duty by his or her act or omission? (the breach question)
> (4) Is the loss for which the claimant seeks damages the consequence of the defendant's act or omission? (the factual causation question)
> (5) Is there a sufficient nexus between a particular element of the harm for which the claimant seeks damages and the subject matter of the defendant's duty of care as analysed at stage 2 above? (the duty nexus question)
> (6) Is a particular element of the harm for which the claimant seeks damages irrecoverable because it is too remote, or because there is a different effective cause (including novus actus interveniens) in relation to it or because the claimant has mitigated his or her loss or has failed to avoid loss.

Lord Leggatt and Lord Burrows agreed in the result, while maintaining a difference of approach (the former maintaining the emphasis on causation and counterfactual analysis and the latter emphasising the role of policy considerations in the scope of the duty of care, with neither endorsing the majority's reformulation of the steps in a negligence claim by the six aforementioned questions).

In *Charles B Lawrence & Associates v Intercommercial Bank Ltd* [2021] UKPC 30; [2022] P.N.L.R. 7, the principles in *Manchester Building Society v Grant Thornton UK LLP* [2021] UKSC 20; [2022] A.C. 783 were applied by the Privy Council in dismissing that part of a claim against a valuer for loss arising from the land in question not having good title, a matter which was held not to be within the purpose of the valuation. At [18]–[19], the Privy Council observed that this was a case where using a "*SAAMCO* counterfactual test" was unhelpful.

Extent of duty—the SAAMCO case

Replace the first paragraph with:

As *Gore Wood (2)*, following the *SAAMCO* [1997] A.C. 191 case, makes clear, **11-13**
and as is implicit in *Caparo v Dickman*, it is not just a question on the facts of any given case whether a duty of care is found to exist, but also the scope of that duty and whether the duty owed was a duty in respect of the kind (not the scale, see *Brown v KMR Services Ltd* [1995] 2 Lloyd's Rep. 513 CA (Civ Div)) of loss of which the victim complains: see, e.g. per Brooke LJ in *Equitable Life Assurance Society v Ernst & Young* [2003] 2 B.C.L.C. 603 at [105].[11] The law as it then stood was summarised in the following passage from the judgment of Arden LJ in *Gore Wood (2)*,[12] but see now *Manchester Building Society v Grant Thornton UK LLP* [2021] UKSC 20; [2022] A.C. 783, noted in para.11-09:

> "91. ... Starting with *Caparo v Dickman*, the courts have moved away from characterising questions of causation and remoteness. The path that once led in that direction now leads in a new direction. The courts now analyse such questions by enquiring whether the duty which the tortfeasor owed was a duty in respect of the kind of loss of which the victim complains. Duty is no longer determined in abstraction from the consequences or vice versa. The same test applies whether the duty of care is contractual or tortious. To determine the scope of the duty the court must examine carefully the purpose for which the advice was given and generally the surrounding circumstances. The determination of the scope of the duty thus involves an intensely fact-sensitive exercise. The final result turns on the facts, and it is likely to be only the general principles rather than the solution in any individual case that are of assistance in later cases."

[11] The "assumption of responsibility" test is also relevant to the issue of remoteness of damage for breach of contract: *Siemens Building Technologies FE Ltd v Supershield Ltd* [2010] 1 Lloyd's Rep. 349.

[12] See also per May LJ in *Sam v Atkins* [2006] R.T.R. 14.

Replace footnote 13 with:

[13] Applied in *Manchester Building Society v Grant Thornton LLP* [2019] EWCA Civ 40, but see now *Manchester Building Society v Grant Thornton UK LLP* [2021] UKSC 20; [2022] A.C. 783, noted in para.11-09.

PIERCING THE CORPORATE VEIL

Equating the company with its shareholders

Replace footnote 16 with:

[16] See also *Brumder v Motornet Service and Repairs Ltd* [2013] 1 W.L.R. 2783. The common law as **11-16**
to the circumstances in which a civil court will stand back from adjudicating a case involving illegality has been radically reshaped in *Patel v Mirza* [2016] UKSC 42; [2017] A.C. 467 (and see further *Stoffel*

& Co v Grondona [2020] UKSC 42; [2021] A.C. 540; *Barrowfen Properties Ltd v Patel* [2021] EWHC 2055 (Ch) at [337]–[340], [684]–[697]).

After the last paragraph, add a new paragraph:

In *Crown Prosecution Service v Aquila Advisory Ltd* [2021] UKSC 49; [2022] B.C.C. 137, the principle in *Bilta* was reaffirmed and it was noted that the principle was unaffected by the Supreme Court's revisiting of the illegality defence in *Patel v Mirza* [2016] UKSC 42; [2017] A.C. 467: the principle in *Bilta* is one of attribution and, if the director(s) illegal conduct cannot be attributed to the company, no defence of illegality against the company's claim can arise.

Shareholder or director's liability for company's costs

To the end of the paragraph, add:

11-17 A convenient summary of the relevant principles is to be found in *Goknur v Aytacli* [2021] EWCA Civ 1037; [2021] B.C.C. 921 at [40]–[41], per Coulson LJ, who concluded that, in practice, an order for costs may be made where either (i) the director (or, potentially, a shareholder) was seeking to benefit personally from the litigation; or (ii) there was impropriety in the conduct of the litigation.

CHAPTER 12

Foreign Element

TABLE OF CONTENTS

ISSUES OF INTERNAL MANAGEMENT—GOVERNED BY LAW OF PLACE OF INCORPORATION

After the first paragraph, add a new paragraph:

As respects forum, this is a basic principle not an absolute rule; in appropriate circumstances, the convenient forum for determining issues of internal management may be found to be other than the place of incorporation such that the courts of another jurisdiction may determine these issues applying the law of the place of incorporation: see, e.g. *KMG International NV v Melanie Anne Chen Chipper Management Ltd* [2018] EWHC 1078 (Comm) at [32]–[36], [95] and *Shallan v Primefuels Investments Ltd* BVIICHMAP2019/005, 18 September 2020 at [37]–[41]. **12-01**

THE EUROPEAN DIMENSION

Replace the first paragraph with:

With the UK's exit from the EU now complete (exit day 31 January 2020 and the transitional period ending 31 December 2020), there is little or no practical distinction between claims involving European entities and other international claims (save, it seems, in respect of proceedings issued before the end of the transitional period as respects, for example, joinder of additional defendants: *Benkel v East-West German Real Estate Holding* [2021] EWHC 188 (Ch); [2021] I.L.Pr. 16). The UK is no longer bound by the Brussels Convention (and the Civil Jurisdiction and Judgments Act 1982 has been amended so as to remove its effect from domestic law). **12-10**

After the first paragraph, add new paragraphs:

The UK had been bound by the Hague Convention by virtue of its EU membership. The UK has now acceded directly to the Hague Convention with effect from 1 January 2021 (i.e. immediately following the end of the transitional period), as reflected by amendments to the 1982 Act made by the Private International Law (Implementation of Agreements) Act 2020. The principal impact of the Hague Convention is to give effect to exclusive choice of court agreements within the scope of the Convention.

Part 6 of the Civil Procedure Rules has been recast to reflect the demise of the previous regime. The main effect is that permission to serve out of the jurisdiction will be needed in most cases where there is no choice of law agreement (whether that is an exclusive choice of court agreement falling within the Hague Convention or another contractual jurisdiction agreement—CPR r.6.33(2B)). CPR r.6.33(3) allows a claim to be served out of the jurisdiction without permission provided that each claim against the defendant is a claim which the court has power to determine (other than under the Hague Convention) notwithstanding that the defendant is abroad and the relevant conduct occurred overseas: this encompasses enactments which on their face contemplate proceedings against persons who are not within the jurisdiction of the court or where the wrongful act, neglect or default giving rise to the claim did not take place within the jurisdiction. Section 994 of the Companies Act 2006 is not such an enactment: see *Re Harrods (Buenos Aires) Ltd* [1992] Ch. 72, CA as respects s.459 of the Companies Act 1985 and R.S.C. Ord. 11 r.1(2)(b), the antecedent of CPR r.6.33(3).

Replace the second paragraph with:

Prior to the UK's exit from the EU, it was necessary to take into account[21] Regulation 44/2001 (the Judgments Regulation)[22] has now largely superseded the Brussels Convention. The Judgments Regulation has direct effect in Member States of the EU (aside from Denmark) and that effect is recognised in Civil Jurisdiction and Judgments Order 2001 (SI 2001/3929) which makes consequential amendments to the Civil Jurisdiction and Judgments Act 1982. For the most part, the jurisdictional rules in the Judgments Regulation reflect the rules in the Brussels and Lugano Conventions, and judicial interpretation of the latter will remain relevant where the Regulation applies. The Lugano Convention continues to apply.

[21] Convention on jurisdiction and the recognition and enforcement of judgments in civil and commercial matters [2007] O.J. L339/3.

[22] Regulation 44/2001 on jurisdiction and the recognition and enforcement of judgments in civil and commercial matters [2001] OJ 12/1.

CHAPTER 13

Miscellaneous Rights

TABLE OF CONTENTS

MERGERS AND CONSOLIDATIONS UNDER CAYMAN ISLANDS LAW

At the end of the last paragraph, replace "Re Qunar Cayman Islands Ltd [2018] 1 CILR 199." with:

Re Qunar Cayman Islands Ltd [2018] 1 CILR 199 (the categories of dissenter disclosure ordered in *Qunar* have been adopted in subsequent cases; in *In the Matter of FGL Holdings and Kingston Partners Master Ltd* 18 December 2020 FSD 0184 OF 2020 (RPJ) and *In the Matter of 58.com* 8 March 2022 FSD 0275 OF 2020 (MRHJ), the Court declined to order disclosure going beyond those categories). **13-05**

After the last paragraph, add a new paragraph:

In the Matter of Nord Anglia Education, INC 17 March 2020 FSD 0235 OF 2017 (IKJ) and *In the matter of Trina Solar Ltd* 23 September 2020 FSD 0092 OF 2017 (NSJ) are instances of substantive judgments on the fair value of shares. In both, the fair value was found to be in excess of the merger price, although in the latter case only marginally so.

INDEX

LEGAL TAXONOMY
FROM SWEET & MAXWELL

This index has been prepared using Sweet & Maxwell's Legal Taxonomy. Main index entries conform to keywords provided by the Legal Taxonomy except where references to specific documents or non-standard terms (denoted by quotation marks) have been included. These keywords provide a means of identifying similar concepts in other Sweet & Maxwell publications and online services to which keywords from the Legal Taxonomy have been applied. Readers may find some minor differences between terms used in the text and those which appear in the index. Suggestions to *sweetandmaxwell.taxonomy@tr.com.*

Also available:

Damages for Breach of Contract, 2nd Edition
Professor Katy Barnett
ISBN: 9780414110878
Publication date: November 2022
Formats: Hardback/ProView eBook
This new work on *Damages for Breach of Contract,* written by new author and Remedies Law leading expert, Professor Katy Barnett, provides authoritative and practical guidance on the nature, extent and limitations of damages individuals and companies can claim in the event of breach of contract.

The book deals primarily with English law, but also considers other jurisdictions (such as Australia and Singapore) when relevant. Clearly setting out what the law is, this new title is written with practitioners in mind. It will also be of real value to students and academics as it considers some of the theoretical debates surrounding this topic

Goff & Jones: The Law of Unjust Enrichment, 10th Edition
Professor Charles Mitchell QC (Hon) FBA, Professor Paul Mitchell and Professor Stephen Watterson
ISBN: 9780414101913
Publication date: November 2022
Formats: Hardback/ProView eBook/Westlaw UK
Goff & Jones is the leading work on the law of unjust enrichment. The new 10th Edition is completely up-to-date and contains detailed discussion of important decisions since the last edition. Several chapters have been wholly or substantially rewritten to take account of significant new cases, and their impact on topics including the recovery of benefits from remote recipients, the recovery of benefits transferred on a condition that fails, the recovery of ultra vires payments by public bodies, the limitation rules governing claims in unjust enrichment and interest awards on such claims.

Contact us: *Tel: +44 (0)345 600 9355* *Order online: sweetandmaxwell.co.uk*

Exclusion Clauses and Unfair Contract Terms, 13th Edition
Professor Neil Andrews
9780414110908
Publication date: November 2022
Formats: Hardback/ProView eBook/Westlaw UK
Fully revised and updated by Professor Neil Andrews to take account of important case law developments of the last five years, *Exclusion Clauses and Unfair Contract Terms* examines, in a detailed, practical, and incisive manner, this important area of contract law. It provides guidance to the practitioner on drafting and using exclusion clauses effectively within the formative phase of a contract. Additionally, it offers commentary on the possibility of challenging an exclusion clause.

Misrepresentation, Mistake and Non-Disclosure, 6th Edition
Professor John Cartwright
ISBN: 9780414089235
Publication date: August 2022
Formats: Hardback/ProView eBook/Westlaw UK
This title explains in detail the doctrines of misrepresentation, mistake and non-disclosure as they affect the validity of contracts. It analyses the consequences of each, focusing in particular on the remedies available to parties in each case.

Fully updated to take account of all the major developments in case law.

Contact us: *Tel: +44 (0)345 600 9355* *Order online: sweetandmaxwell.co.uk*

ProView

THIS TITLE IS NOW AVAILABLE DIGITALLY

Thomson Reuters ProView

The Premier eBook experience for professionals worldwide via your browser, tablet or smartphone

For further information about purchase or multi-user options please select **Print and ProView eBook Services** in **Contact us** at www.tr.com/uki-legal-contact, call 0345 600 9355, or contact your trade agent

THOMSON REUTERS®